CELEBRATION OF LIFE

BARRY PRIVETT

Author Help

In memory of my amazing parents Ruby & Len and two special friends, Coxy & Jimmy Banks.

I
PRELUDE

I was originally going to call this book "101 Snippets Of My Life" because that's all it is but, when Jacky came across the photo which was taken on my 70th birthday and is on the front cover with the banner over my head, "CELEBRATION OF LIFE", that sums it up.

My father didn't talk much about his life and talking with friends I discovered they also didn't know much about their fathers' lives. So, I decided to break from tradition and spill the beans, warts and all.

So here I am seventy-two years young, I say young as I still feel that age is only a number, I am still healthy and got all my faculties. Yes, I have all the expected aches and pains and I know I will never run in a marathon again nor score the winning try for Exeter Chiefs, but I have had a life full of memories.

I have been blessed with three fantastic children and six beautiful grandchildren, what more could I want? Taken from a song from The Who, "I was born with a plastic spoon in my mouth" but slowly over the years built up quite a portfolio and find myself not wanting for anything. Taken from another song, this time Frank Sinatra, "regrets I've had a few but too few to mention" I have a philosophy on life and that is regret things you have done, not things you haven't done. Hindsight is a totally different kettle of fish and if I had known what I know now when I bought my first house at the age of nineteen, I would've bought the whole street.

SINCE THE AGE OF THIRTEEN I HAVE NEVER HAD CHRISTMAS Day off, as from thirteen to eighteen years of age I worked all holidays in a hotel and from the age of eighteen to thirty-three played keyboards in other hotels, from thirty-three always went into the care home. My Christmas Day would be up at 8 am, move equipment from the hotel I played in the night before, after that over to the care home to distribute gifts and help serve lunch, then back to a different hotel to set the equipment up, home by 4 pm for dinner and time with the children, then off again at 7 pm to play keyboard until midnight. Perhaps next year could be my first Christmas off.

When I was young, I missed out on a number of social gatherings but I have no regrets. Occasionally I get people say to me, "It's alright for you", which I detest hearing. Perhaps after reading this book of "snippets" they might change their mind.

2

EARLY LIFE

I have very little recollection of my infant school days. I was born on the 26th of October 1948 in Torbay Hospital, the third child of my parents Ruby and Len. My elder brother Roger was seven years old then and my elder sister Julie was fifteen months older than me and still is! In 1956 my younger sister Dawn was born. We all lived in a terraced house at 19 Belmont Road which was actually in Ellacombe but Belmont Road was bisected by Carlton Road and the east part was in Babbacombe and the west part, in which 19 was situated, was in Ellacombe. Babbacombe was a more select area so although number 19 was in the west side mother, who was a bit of a snob, would always say we lived in Babbacombe. We were blessed with a variety of shops all around us. At the end of the road was a Co-Op which later in life I would go to with a list of shopping and hand it to the shopkeeper, including on a good day broken biscuits and five Woodbine for dad. There was a separate counter opposite for bacon, ham, cheese etc. They would cut the bacon with a huge razor-sharp wheel which spun round with a little safety device. Mum had a Co-Op divi number 3285, from which she would occasionally get some kind of reward. Next door was the Co-Op butcher with all the fresh meat hanging in the window and sawdust on the floor. Across the road was what we called the tin shop where we would go for paraffin for our heaters at home, further on from there were two more shops, one of which was my favourite because they only sold sweets. The other way was the post office, a wool shop, a newsagent and a corner shop. Around the other corner was a dairy, a hairdresser, and a corner shop. Sadly, all these have now gone except the corner shop past the post office which is now a small supermarket.

My first school was Homelands Infants of which I have truly little memory except each afternoon we had to get the sponge mats out to lie on for an afternoon nap, and in the morning we were given a small bottle of milk to drink and every week we had a spoonful of cod-liver oil, yuck!!

My father didn't talk much about his early days except during the war for a while he was sent to India and was involved in operating searchlights to spot enemy planes. He was a painter and decorator by trade and every Thursday would hand his unopened wage packet to my mother who would return him some spending money. He did tell me a story once about how, along with some others they were decorating a very posh house when someone knocked over a tin of paint onto the carpet. They quickly grabbed the pet dog, put some paint on its tail and told the owner the dog had knocked the tin over.

One thing I did enjoy was a radio programme every Saturday morning called Listen with Mother. I would sit on the kitchen step and no one was allowed to talk whilst it was on.

Although we lived in a small three-bedroomed terraced house mother took in paying guests. I can't remember how many, but I know our dining room was full so it must have been about sixteen. They would have a cooked breakfast, come back for a roast dinner, then back again at 5:30 for a cooked tea. Hardly any had cars so they would bus or walk everywhere.

Goodness knows how they did it or how they ate so much food, but the same guests came back year after year. The guests' sleeping arrangements were strange, some were accommodated at our house and the rest slept in homes down and across the road. This meant that mum and dad slept in a put-you-up bed in the kitchen and my sister and I moved into the garden shed in bunk beds.

By now my brother had joined the merchant navy so we saw very little of him, however he had his own shed and he said he wouldn't be home much more which disappointed me because I used to enjoy it when he came home. We would play fight and he would always let me win. He once set up a boxing ring in the garden and started to teach me how to box. He did a little boxing himself but after his first fight came home claiming that his opponent had punched him on the nose.

Now I had a school friend whose father kept racing pigeons and he asked if I would like some. I went straight home and asked if I could keep racing pigeons in my brother's shed and surprisingly my parents agreed. I spent hours making perches, nest boxes etc and when it was all ready got my racing pigeons. When we went to get the pigeons my friend's father had left us a note asking us to kill three of his chickens. We thought that would be no problem until we tried it. We were told to put their heads on a block and strike heavily with a piece of 3 x 2 wood. No one was brave enough to do it, we each gave the chickens a little tap, they gave out a little cluck, but nothing happened, so we took them down to the butcher to do the deed. When my friend's father found them he congratulated us on being so brave. We never told him the butcher did it.

MY FRIEND'S FATHER HAD EXPLAINED TO ME THAT EVERY time I fed the pigeons I should bang loudly on a saucepan and they would know it was feeding time and if they were out flying around, they would come back. Every day for six weeks when I fed them, I religiously banged on the saucepan and then felt it was safe to let them out, which I did. An hour or so later I went out banging on my saucepan but never saw them again.

Now at eight years old I had a particularly good friend called Jeff who lived up the road. His father was a signwriter and outside his workshop on the wall had an advert for a local cinema called the Regal, for this he was given two complimentary tickets per week for the cinema and Jeff and I would go regularly. A little later I would go to Saturday morning pictures at the Regal Cinema which was opposite the Town Hall in Torquay. There would be a cartoon on then a support film then the main film, these of course would all be in black and white. All this for six old pence equivalent to two and a half new pence. There was always a huge girl called Hilda who came from Watcombe, she was built like the proverbial S.H. with no teeth, if she wanted to sit where you were you would always move and if there was a fight Hilda was always involved.

It was with Jeff that I first ventured into being an entrepreneur. We made a go-kart out of three planks of wood with wheels in the four corners. It had no brakes, and the front plank was on a fulcrum so you could steer it. We came up with the idea that if we had a trailer, we could go to the neighbours offering a rubbish clearance service. So, we set about building a trailer and when we had finished we put written flyers through neighbours' doors and surprise surprise we got a job. A neighbour had just finished demolishing a wall and offered us seven shillings and sixpence [37p] to take all the stones up to the tip. The tip was about a mile away and we thought it would take four or five trips, so we accepted the job. Now the trailer was made out of planks of wood with a wheel on each corner and an old zinc bath on the top to carry the rubbish. We completed the first run which probably took two hours and came back and filled our zinc bath with the second load when disaster struck. We were halfway to the tip, which was then situated near Walls Hill in Babbacombe, when the wheels on the trailer buckled and broke, and when we tried to pull the zinc bath the bottom came off. We carefully placed the stones on the grass verge, took our go-kart and broken trailer back home and put a note through my neighbour's door saying that we were sorry we were unable to fulfil this contract.

WE NEVER HAD PROPER FAMILY HOLIDAYS EXCEPT DURING the summer when sometimes we would go and see our uncles and aunts in Cheltenham, this was usually just me and my sister but occasionally mum came with us. If she drove us there it would take her all day, stopping near Exeter for a picnic breakfast, then Taunton for lunch and arriving at Cheltenham in the early evening. Mum was such a slow driver later she took Julie, me and the girl across the road to our first pop concert in Exeter. It was Gene Pitney supported by Cliff Richard and the Shadows, and on the way back she was stopped by the police for driving too slowly.

Most of the time we would be sent to Cheltenham on our own by train and I remember one trip where Julie and I sat on a box in the guard's van with the guard keeping an eye on us. My uncle had the first television I saw, and it was in a huge cabinet probably three feet high by two feet wide but the black and white television which only showed one very snowy channel was only about eight inches in the middle. My aunt and uncle also made us go to Sunday school which was a long trek down lanes to get to which I didn't enjoy. Once they sent us home early, I assume for misbehaving but I don't recall the reason.

On one other occasion as a family, we went to London for a few days which was so exciting. We stayed in a guesthouse which was about six stories high but only two bathrooms. I doubt if there were any fire regulations at this time. The highlight of this trip was when dad took me to the motor show, although we also went to Madame Tussauds.

During this time, I was an enthusiastic member of the 20th Sea Scouts as a Cub Scout and we met every Friday at the Scout hall which was where The Range is now. I later became a full Scout and stayed with the Sea Scouts for eight years during which time we would go out in the bay in our canoes and one day a full-size basking shark swam right up close to us. We would fish for mackerel which was so plentiful I would throw a line out with six hooks on it and within minutes haul in six mackerel.

I also became a member of the Gang Show, which was made up of Boy and Cub Scouts, we would rehearse every week in rooms in Rock Road. My mother got involved in making costumes. We would do sketches like one where we all dressed up as nursery rhyme figures, I was Old Mother Hubbard, and the song went like this:

Nursery rhymes and fairy tales
Are just a lot of hairy tales
No secrets more to hold
Let at last the truth be told

We all sang this together and then it was my turn to sing on my own, my line went something like this:

In my cupboard I declare
I never ever found it bare
Old mother Hubbard knew she'd got
A nice little bottle of you know what

I would then bring out a bottle of beer and on the last night I opened it and took a swig and spat it out saying it was horrible, this was picked up on the microphone which caused hysterics in the audience. Another character was The Doctor with a little black bag and there were others, but my memory fails me. We played at the Pavilion for a full week and on Thursdays, Fridays and Saturdays it was always a sell-out. We then moved to the Princess Theatre, being the first amateur show there. One night after the show I was just climbing the stairs beside the stage when someone turned the lights out and I fell into the orchestra pit and was taken to hospital with concussion. Anyway, I was in the gang show for eight consecutive years from the age of eight to sixteen years old and I loved every minute.

Of course, being a Boy Scout involved Bob a job week. For younger readers this meant going around the houses asking if anyone had a job they wanted doing for which they would give me a bob, a bob is slang for one shilling old money which is 5p in new money, all the money went to the Scouts' charity. I didn't particularly like doing this as some people would take advantage and get you weeding the garden for two hours, however one lady would always give me two shillings and a banana and never asked me to do anything. Later when I became a Scout, in order to obtain my first class badge, I had to hike out on Dartmoor with a colleague and pitch up a tent to stay overnight, so we set out with a backpack, a tent and a compass. A thick fog descended, and we couldn't see our hand in front of our face, and we were completely lost so we decided we would pitch the tent and continue in the morning. When we woke up in the morning, we found we had pitched the tent in the middle of a traffic island.

By now I had moved to Ellacombe primary school and in my early days was quite a bright student but slowly deteriorated over the years. When you got to primary school you had already been graded and if you were quite bright you were put in the even number classes and others put in the odd number. I went into form two then four then six but in six they found I was finding it too easy, so I was taken out and accelerated to form eight. The trouble was I was too young to take the 11+ so had to stay in form eight for two years and when I took the 11+ exam I thought it was a joke, I wouldn't be surprised if I got 100%. It continued at the grammar school where the forms were A, B, C and D depending how well you did in the 11+. I went to form 1A then 2X, the X stood for extreme, the idea was that I was going to miss out year 3, go straight to year 4, and take my O-levels a year early. However, things started to go wrong in year 2X and I went on to 3B then 4C then 5D. Each year after the end of terms one and three we had to take an exam, now in my opinion they were just glorified memory tests which I wasn't very good at. In term two you were just assessed on your casework. Whilst in term one and three my form position was always in the high 20s out of 34, in term two I would be in the top ten and in fact once in term two I finished first. Despite this, in that term report there was still a comment that I could do better.

Anyway, back to my primary school days. We only had two tarmac playgrounds, one for boys and one for girls, we had to walk half a mile to Brewery Park for any sports. I was quite a good sportsman, always scoring the most runs at rounders, coming first in all the races and the long jump, but never did well in the high jump, I wonder why and when we played basketball, I was always last to be picked.

During school holidays me and my mates would go down to the beach, change into our swimming costume and go off for the day. Then one day we were gone for so long the tide had come in and washed all our clothes away. I wasn't the most popular with my mum. Another day playing football in a very muddy field I went home covered head to toe in mud, frightened what my mum would say, but she just laughed at me and fetched the neighbour in to see such a sorry sight. Much laughter ensued.

Eating at home was not pleasant, occasionally we would have pork knuckles which were pigs' trotters. When mother boiled them the whole house would smell, usually the home would constantly smell of tea as both Mum and Dad were big tea drinkers. Perhaps that is why I hate tea to this day. Also, when she cooked fish it was never filleted and I would spend most of my mealtime picking the bones out of my mouth and occasionally swallowing one, that is probably why I still dislike fish. When we sat down to eat both Mum and Dad had loose fitting dentures and they would make a dreadful noise clacking as they ate. My sister would eat her meals very quickly so as to get away from the table. Even to this day she still eats very quickly.

If mum was annoyed with us and we were playing downstairs in the cellar she would pretend to faint and make a big bang as she hit the floor so we would run upstairs. If we weren't in the cellar and she was annoyed with us she would put her coat on and say "I'm off, leaving you all" and then walk up to the Co-op at the end of the road, and wait there until one of us went up to apologise and ask her to come home. On saying this, I dearly loved my mother and father, not really realising at the time what they went through in order to feed us and keep us safe.

Once on April 1st I phoned mum up pretending I was a lorry driver and had a pallet full of tins of prunes and asked her where she wanted them left. Of course my mum said she didn't order them. I told her I was going to deliver them anyway and leave them in the front garden. At this she went berserk shouting down the phone, and I put my phone down. A few hours later when I came home I couldn't help coming in with a big smile on my face. Mum took one look at me and shouted "It was you".

My Grandmother sitting on her Grandmothers knee circa 1890

My FathersParents

My Grandmother &Step Grandfather

A young Mum &Dad

All my Aunts & Uncles with my Grandmother

3
ADOLESCENCE

I think my love for music started around this time as I would religiously listen to radio Luxembourg and spend hours soaking in the bath listening to it. I remember they used to have an advert called Horace Bachelor's Infra-Draw Method, he was from Keynsham in Bristol. It was some scheme to help you win the pools (before the lottery you tried to predict football scores and if you got eight out of eight you could win tens of thousands of pounds) I used to think to myself if he used the scheme on himself, he would be a millionaire.

I bought my first record, "Tell Laura I love her" by Rickie Valance, which I would play constantly on my Dancette record player, to this day I know every word. Another early record was "Let there be drums" by Sandy Nelson, which was given to me as a birthday present by my mate Jeff and as he was quite artistic had meticulously created his own artwork on the cover.

When I was 11 there was a girl in my last year of primary school who I was going to marry. Her name was Linda, occasionally on my way home from scouts on a Friday night I would throw a little gravel up to her bedroom window and she would open her curtains and give me a wave. Then on Saturday morning I would meet her on Devon Road and for half an hour we would just walk around Cary Park. After about four or five weeks I asked her if I could give her a kiss, so we went into the washroom area of the park ladies' toilets. I was just summing up the courage to give her a kiss when the door opened and in walked a policeman. Needless to say, we were both petrified as in those days you had upmost respect for the police. He asked me what we were doing and with my bottom lip trembling I stammered that I was going to give my girl-friend a kiss. "And also what are you going to do?" the policeman asked. I had no idea what he meant so just said "nothing officer", it wasn't until a couple of years later I realised what he meant. How the innocent times have changed. I often wonder what happened to Linda as I never saw her again after I left primary school.

Me and my mates would also go up into the woods at the top of Windsor Road and spend hours seeing what we could find. One day we decided to have a fire and cook some sausages. We used an old enamel tray as the frying pan but didn't realise the heat would loosen the paint and it stuck onto the sausages. So, we ate the sausages paint and all.

If we didn't have anything to do on a Saturday Jeff and I would try hitch-hiking just to see how far we could get. I remember once getting as far as Haytor and another time to Lustleigh. When we were picked up by a Rolls-Royce it was the first time I had travelled at 100 mph. No way would eleven or twelve year olds be allowed or want to do that these days.

At twelve years old my parents could not afford to give me any pocket money, so I got a paper round. Every day including Sunday I would deliver papers from Hatfield Cross down the St Marychurch Road and up Ash Hill Road. Once a month one customer had a magazine called Health and Efficiency delivered with his paper, this magazine was, so I am told, a magazine for naturalists including photos. One month he didn't receive it and all hell broke loose. I assume I had delivered to the wrong address, however nobody ever admitted receiving it. I was paid eleven shillings per week for this which today is 55p but after a while all the paperboys went on strike and he increased our wage to twelve shillings and sixpence (62p).

Also around this time I became a member of the Upton church choir but didn't particularly enjoy it, I believe it was mother's idea for me to join as my grandmother was a regular part of the church congregation. This didn't last very long as not only did I not enjoy it but I wasn't a very good singer.

It was nice to have some money which I had earned myself as a few years earlier my uncle would occasionally call and throw pennies, half pennies and farthings over the kitchen floor and watch me and my sister scramble around to find them. At the time we thought it was fun but looking back it was a rather arrogant thing for him to do. When I was fourteen, I had saved up through working and bought a bike. After leaving it in the cellar for a while, when I got it out I found the frame was cracked and it would cost £11 to repair which I did not have. I was in our dining room with the serving hatch open when I heard my mother talking to that same uncle and telling him that when he pulled my bike out, he cracked the frame. Neither of them ever admitted this to me, although I never blamed my mother. But my uncle who enjoyed throwing the pennies around could have helped, after all I was only fourteen.

At the age of thirteen I walked down to the Palace Hotel in Torquay and asked if they had any jobs going. They asked me how old I was, and I told them I was fourteen. They said I could start as a commie waiter, (for those who don't know the commie waiter is a gofer for the waiter) my hours were 7 am to 10:30 am, then 12 till 3 pm then 6 till I had finished, usually between 9 and 10pm, 6 days a week. After meals I had to tidy up around my designated tables, hoover up, then layup the tables ready for the next meal. It didn't dawn on me to ask how much I was being paid but at the end of the first week when I was paid £4, I was delighted. Even more delighted when at the end of the second week a guest gave me £4 as a tip.

After serving these seven course meals the food we had was poor, sausage and mash or soggy cottage pie. I was reprimanded one day for having three Weetabix for breakfast instead of two even though I never had a cooked breakfast. Some of the waiters would order one of the same meals the guests were having for themselves and hide it underneath the station (this was the table they serve the meals from) but the head waiter got wise to this and would check under the bottom shelf. However, one waiter went a step too far as his wife ran a small guesthouse for six to eight guests and whatever we had at the hotel in the evening they would have the next day. Of course he was caught and fired. Another firing took place which I found very funny. You have to remember all the guests got dressed up for dinner, usually dinner suits and long dresses for the ladies and the better the bedroom you had booked then the better the table you had in the restaurant. If you had a table overlooking the gardens you had one of the full-time experienced waiters. All the others were down the far end of the dining room and were dealt with by the Irish waiters who just came in for the summer, which we called the cowboy waiters. Then during dinner one evening Harry Evans would play the piano accompanied by an oboe player and a violinist, they would just play quiet background music. One evening a cowboy waiter was passing a table and took some sauce off it, the guest shouted that he had not finished with it, but the waiter ignored him. The fiery guest chased after him and a fight took place in the middle of the dining room. Harry Evans saw what was going on and broke into the William Tell overture "DIDDLE UM DIDDLE UM DIDDLE UM DUM DUM". They finished off in the kitchen and the waiter was sacked. We had a few celebrities stay, they included The Walker Brothers, Steptoe and son, and Billy J

Kramer (who gave me tickets for his show, but I was working).

As I said I saved all my wages to buy the bike, it was a long walk to and from the hotel. I carried on working at the Palace Hotel during all my school holidays and occasionally for functions and after a while they made me up to a proper waiter earning £20 a week and sometimes my share of the 10% service charge that was added to the guest bill was as much as £20 per week, but this was only for a few weeks a year. After this I moved to The Warberry Hotel but that was only for one season.

Whilst I was at grammar school I still enjoyed my sports, even though I struggled academically as mentioned earlier. I was good at cross country running and if I wanted to get home early I would come in the top three when we had races. If I didn't want to get home early I would stay back with my mates who would hide behind a bush for a fag and join up with the others when they came round on the second lap, I never tried cigarettes at this age but I did for a few years later.

I was always picked for the school rugby team. In those days one of the smallest players was picked as the hooker, which was me, but nearly always finished with a bleeding nose as someone would punch me in the scrums, so I changed to scrum-half which I thoroughly enjoyed, receiving the school colours. I also played for Torquay Tics under 16s for one year before I broke my leg.

Throughout my life I have really enjoyed all kinds of sport but never achieved dizzy heights in any of them. In football I played for St Marychurch Spurs and Watts Blake & Bearne, but was always picked for the second team and the nearest I got to scoring a hat-trick was when, after I had already scored two goals, I was pushed in the penalty area, but the captain wouldn't let me take the resulting penalty. We played at some isolated places, one in particular down in the South Hams where we all had to change in a garage. After the match we were given a tin bath full of cold water to wash in, all twenty-two of us.

Talking of football, I turned out for my pub for a charity match and I was told we should all dress in ladies clothing. When I got there, I was the only one wearing ladies clothing, but it was under my tracksuit. I was so embarrassed I played the whole match with my tracksuit on.

Continuing with my sporting achievements, or lack of, I played cricket in a business league, 20/20 games, my best score was forty-six. On the last game I had we were having difficulty getting one of the good opposition players out, so the captain asked me to bowl. I clean bowled the batsman out first ball. Unfortunately this was followed with three wides, so the captain took me off. I did however get many players out during the fifteen years I played. I was in my fifties when I played my last rugby match, when I turned out for Torquay Veterans. The team we played against didn't have many veterans in it, in fact my opposite number still hadn't started to shave. We were just pipped 46-0.

Both Daniel and Ben were good rugby players and I followed them to nearly all their games, both home and away. At Bovey Tracey Dan got into a skirmish with one of their players and being the only away supporter, I tried to sort it out only to see about twenty of their supporters descending on me. However, I survived. The only time I ever ran on the pitch was when Ben had his head stamped on. I remonstrated with the referee and was told to get off the pitch. Luckily, their coach saw the incident and took his own player off.

Another time I was looking out for Ben was on his eighteenth birthday. Ben had quite rightly punched a boy for inappropriately touching his then girlfriend. The bouncers were in the throes of throwing Ben out when I intervened and I, in my late fifties, got thrown out as well. Although putting myself down as a sportsman I recently disposed of at least thirty trophies I had accumulated over the years. They were for football, cricket, squash, racquet ball, golf and even one for tennis. The tennis trophy was for the South West England civil service mixed doubles and the only reason we won it was because in mixed doubles they always played to the lady assuming she was the weakest player and we were always one set up before the opponents realised I was the weaker player.

I had saved up by the time I was sixteen to buy a second-hand scooter which was a Lambretta TV175 with chrome sides and chrome bars everywhere. It was on this scooter I had an accident and broke my leg. I don't know how I did it, but I hit a parked car in Lymington Road, I think it must've jumped out at me. I had a plaster from my toes to the top of my leg, my leg itched to such an extent I had to push a knitting needle down the top of the plaster to alleviate the itching. I was in plaster for four months and when I had the plaster removed my leg was bent, I remember the original surgeon saying "Oh no not another scooter accident" which didn't give me much faith in him.

I went to physiotherapy for a while and the day the physio told me to try walking without a stick the surgeon called me in and said my leg had not set properly and I had two choices firstly to carry on, but I would probably get arthritis in my forties, or secondly have it broken and start all over again. I chose option two and subsequently was sent to Exeter hospital to have it re-broken and start all over. This time it was much better, and I could weightbear after two months although the plaster stayed on for a further four months.

It was during this time I was playing with a ball on the beach when a boxer dog bit and burst the ball, then turned on me although I was not injured, from that day on I have been wary of big dogs.

Being in plaster for so long had a profound effect on my schoolwork. I had achieved six O-levels and was in the sixth form studying A-levels in pure maths, applied maths, and art as I had set my mind on being an architect. At the end of the first year, I was really struggling with my maths because I had so much time off due to my broken leg and so I went to see the headmaster for some advice. His response was you can take the year again, you can struggle on, or you can leave there's the door. How times have changed. Anyway, I left.

At the grammar school they still had corporal punishment and detention. I was once put in detention for being seen a mile away from school not wearing my school cap. Most teachers had their own way of giving out punishment, the head used the cane, the sports master a very worn plimsoll, maths the side of the ruler over your knuckles or a clip round the ear, Latin a wooden backed blackboard duster thrown at you, but the worst was the art teacher. He would bend you over a chair in front of the class and run at you with a leather strap and give you three strokes. One boy was seen to be grinning at his mates after the beating and was brought back by the teacher and beaten until he cried.

My history teacher, with the unfortunate name of Mr Kneebone, was so lazy he would just say open your book at a certain page and read, which we did until the bell went. He didn't teach us anything.

Me

19 Belmont Road

Carrying Dawn in front of my bedroom

Mum Dad & Roger

Moving on to Infants School

4
AND SO TO WORK

So I left school and queued up at the dole office, to my surprise one day my ex-maths master was also queueing up. Apparently he had been sacked for clipping a boy around the ear who had just had an operation to pin his ears back. Being on the dole was no fun, no money, boring days. Anyway me and my mate Dave would help a wrestling promoter who would put on wrestling bouts. Town halls, village halls, church halls, everywhere, he would advertise it as a full evening of wrestling but in fact he would only use four wrestlers. The first fight would be A versus B, second fight C versus D, third fight would be the masked warrior which was A with a mask on and he would fight either C or D, then a tag match which was two against two which was A and B versus C and D. One night when a wrestler was supposedly unconscious, I had to go on with my bucket and sponge. He opened one eye and said to me "Blonde three rows back on the right, ask her what she is doing afterwards" then slipped back into his supposed unconsciousness.

Also, at that time I did a fair bit of oil paintings and in fact had three of my paintings exhibited in an art exhibition.

So now it was time for me to get a proper job, I went to a

company called Sifams Ltd who made calibrating instruments, being paid £8 per week. After six or seven months they offered me a sandwich course which meant I spent six months per year at university and six months a year working at Sifams for three years. However, I enquired what would happen after three years and they told me that if I didn't get the correct grades they would try and find me a job on the shop floor, if I did get the correct grades, they expected me to stay with them for at least a further three years. As I didn't like these conditions I left. One thing I do remember was whilst there I was drilling some hard metal when the drill bit snapped and the metal flew across the workshop floor and hit this six-foot rugby player and he fell to the floor as though he'd been shot. He recovered okay but on reflection I found it quite funny. He is now the radio commentator for Exeter Chiefs.

I already had a job lined up for when I left, as a tax officer working for the Inland Revenue in Torquay for £7 a week.

By now I was dating Jackie who I met at St Marychurch youth club, I remember the first dance I had with her the group were playing The House of the Rising Sun. We dated for many years and not long before we got married, we went on a holiday to Ibiza. I had been to France on a day trip once before on a ferry that used to run from Torquay, I had a free ticket because my parents advertised it in their little guest house. I also had been to Lisbon and Madeira which was a school cruise trip on a converted warship called The Devonian which was extremely basic sleeping in dormitories ten to a room. During our day's stop in Lisbon three of us were arrested for wearing shorts in the city centre and taken to the police station where we were kept for many hours and only had food and drink which we bought from a street trader who had been arrested for operating without a license. As none of us could speak Portuguese and none of the police could speak English, they released us and took us back to the ship but made us cover our legs with the police issue macs while we were walking up the gangplank, I was only fifteen at the time.

Back to our holiday in Ibiza, we stayed in a basic hotel in San Antonio, which at that time wasn't much more than a large village. They had a happy hour each evening when the barman would just walk away from the bar and say help yourself, for the next hour free of charge, we all did. Our bedroom was across the road, it took us ages to find these rooms. On one evening out, neither of us knowing much about Spanish food, we thought we would order something very Spanish. Bearing in mind I don't like to eat fish, we ordered a large bowl of paella, needless to say I went hungry. Something similar happened when we first got married and ordered our first Chinese takeaway. Not knowing what we had ordered we found the first two courses were just full of noodles, never mind I said we have a nice desert, pancake rolls! of course they were also full of noodles.

After that slight diversion I will go back to my late teens. I had a good friend called Tony who played in a pop group and I found myself going around with them and helping set up equipment etc. I got the bug and went to Exeter and bought a Vox Continental electric organ for £108 on higher purchase and had to pay back £2 something a week for a year. I learnt all the basic chords and a few other notes and joined the group. Although I got up to an acceptable standard, I never classed myself as a musician and on my tax return for many years I referred myself as an entertainer, not a musician. The group was called The Sixth Sense and we did have some early changes in personnel and finished up with Phil Bristow lead guitar, Tony Brinsley bass, Dave Klingenberg drums, myself on keyboard and Davy Jones singer (not the Davy Jones from the Monkeys). Playing village and town halls in Devon some events which stick in my mind.

Playing Bovey Tracey Town Hall our agent Lionel Digby had seen the smoke effect that The Who had used so he thought we should replicate it. Not having any dry ice, he turned up with sticks that looked like dynamite. They were in fact drain clearance sticks which the council workmen would light and put down a drain and if the smoke came up the next drain, they knew they were clear. Lionel lit one on the front of the stage, within two minutes the whole hall was so thick with smoke you couldn't see your hand in front of your face. The whole place had to be evacuated and an ambulance was called for a lady who suffered with asthma.

On another occasion, funnily enough the same venue, it was decided to have a themed effect on our show and the theme was the evils of television. Near the end of our show Phil was really going to town on his guitar when a TV was brought onto the stage and myself and Davy promptly started to chop it up with a 7-pound axe. Unfortunately, we didn't realise there was a number of well-known gypsies in the audience and as bits came off the TV, they started throwing them back at us. This got so dangerous we stopped playing and hid behind our equipment, trouble was we left the axes on the stage and the gypsies started to chop up the stage. The police were called, calmed everything down and left, leaving us to start playing again. Next problem when the gypsies started to chop up the stage they chopped through our cables and so we couldn't play, another riot ensued, and the police were called again. This event made headlines in the South Devon Journal with the heading "TV Axing was only a Gimmick".

We were asked if we would like to do a three-night tour of South Wales which we agreed to, the only trouble was that Tony our bass player could not make it. So Phil showed me the rudiments of bass playing and off we went with me attempting to play bass. There was a piece in the evening paper because we were the first group to cross the new Severn Bridge. One night playing at a rugby club we were offered a green and brown pill being told it would make us feel good, so Phil and I tried one and played that night. Afterwards I asked Phil if it made him feel any different to which he said no and nor did it me, however as we couldn't afford hotels, we all slept in the van in the rugby club carpark. About three or four in the morning I felt the van shaking, I could hear banging and see flashing lights. I thought to myself what had these pills done to me then the door of the van opened and it was the police checking on us and the shaking and banging was the policeman trying to wake us and the flashing light was on top of the police car. This frightened me so much I never experimented with anything again although I had plenty of offers.

After every gig we did we were paid and when we deducted petrol money and had our two or three quid each, we never kept any money to pay our agent his 10%. He used to bring well-known groups down to the town hall in Torquay and we would go on as a support act, to cover his non-payment of commission we played for free. Some of the bands we supported were The Who, Slade, Lindisfarne, The Kinks, The Love Affair, The Equals (when Eddie Grant was with them), Cream who were made up of Jack Bruce, Ginger Baker and Eric Clapton. They just wanted a warm up gig in a small town before they went on a world tour. When Amen Corner were on their way down their vehicle broke down the other side of Newton Abbot, so we went to pick them and their equipment up. As a thank you they let us use all their equipment and it was the first time I ever played a Hammond organ. The Rolling Stones also came down, but they did not want a support act.

Most of the groups were particularly good but when we played "Baby come back" which was a number one song by The Equals we got a bigger round of applause than The Equals did. The bar at the town hall was downstairs and when the main band was on those in the bar would all come upstairs, however when The Love Affair started playing, they were so bad after two songs everyone went back down again.

We played at the town hall so often that the agent/promoter suggested we used different names when we were advertised as a support group, my favourite was Felicity Bucket's Imaginary Menagerie. This name was derived from when our guitarist Phil swore, and his father overheard him. Phil told him that he had said bucket so Phil became Felicity and hence the name Felicity's Buckets and we just added the Imaginary Menagerie.

In the hope I could make a little extra money I had my name down with the town hall security team as a bouncer when I wasn't playing there. Due to me not being the perfect size for a bouncer I never expected a call, then to my surprise they did call me, and I went down only to find The Wurzels were playing there and I was in charge of crowd control of twenty blue rinse elderly ladies.

Every year Lionel the promoter would bring down other groups from up country for a whole week and pay them £100 for the week and then send them out each night to play at different venues around the west country, mainly village halls. One group he had who had signed a contract a few months previously were playing at the village hall in Lustleigh, on the same day they had reached number one in the charts, but they had to still fulfil that contract. When the Beatles came back from Hamburg, he was offered them but he turned them down because they wanted £150 for the week.

We would regularly go down to Cornwall and the Pink Flamingo was one of the places we would play. It was a massive hall, now a supermarket, on the Saturday night supporting well-known bands of that time Herman's Hermits, The Merseybeats, Geno Washington and the Ram Jam Band to name a few. We would stay overnight in the attached motel, then on Sunday they would bring a partition halfway across the hall and we played again, this time on our own then packed up and at about 4 am set off home. Our van was so old and slow it took forever to get home, I had to start work at 8 am, quite often I went straight there.

One night at the Pink Flamingo the bar manager gave us a bottle of whisky and me and Tony who roomed together had a drinking competition. All I remember was that I wet the bed and when I told Tony he walked down the corridor and flushed the toilet. Tony never touched alcohol again after this incident.

When we came back from gigs in Devon, we would often stop at a place we called Dirty Dots which was the most disgusting café you could imagine in Exeter, but late at night it was the only café open. We would ask for a fried breakfast without, when Dot asked without what we would say without swimming in fat. Another place where we stopped was Peamore Garage which was just before Telegraph Hill, whilst not open the vending machine did a very nice soup. We often met other groups there and all raced back to Torquay, no dual carriageway in those days. One of our main competitors was a group called The Empty Vessels who later became Wishbone Ash. The problem we had was that our van could not get up Telegraph Hill fully laden, so Dave who is quite a big lad, had to get out and walk and I would keep him company. We would always stop and have a chat with Old Smokey, a tramp who lived part way up the hill.

Another group who were due to play in Cornwall didn't have a van so they borrowed ours which had our name on the side. The group were so bad they were banned from playing there again but everyone thought it was us, so we got banned from this place without going near it.

I was told when I was younger, I looked a little like Dudley Moore and in fact once met Peter Cook in a Torquay night club and asked him and he said I looked more like Dudley Moore than ******* Dudley Moore did. Once a girl ran across the street, looked me straight in the eye and shouted to her friend “no it’s not“ and ran off again. Later in life I now get comments that I look like David Jason.

When I was nineteen, I bought my first house in Ellacombe Church Road. I took six months looking for a house I could turn into three flats. One I looked at was up for sale for £3,400 but it was cheap because it had a sitting tenant in it. Walking down the street a week or two later I met a lady who used to live in this property, she stopped me and told me the sitting tenant had died. I went straight down to the estate agent and offered the full £3,400 and was surprised they accepted; the only problem was I only had £400. I approached the bank and told them I was going to live there in the property and could they lend me £3,000. The manager said he would come and look, so I promptly borrowed the key to the house and converted it overnight by stripping one of the upstairs kitchens back into a bedroom. The bank manager called and agreed the loan, the problem now was I could not afford the first month's bank payment so I worked every hour for weeks. In fact one day I got a knock on the door, and a neighbour asked me if I could be a little quieter. I said sorry I didn't realise you had gone to bed to which he replied it's 4 o'clock in the morning. I completed the top two floors into flats by the end of the first month and rented them out at £6 a week with a £6 deposit which was enough to pay the first month's payment to the bank. I was so exhausted that it was another month before I converted the garden rooms into a flat.

During this time, I was still working at the Inland Revenue and in fact took an exam to become a tax officer higher grade. Which I subsequently passed and got promoted. I still wasn't enamoured with this job, but it paid its way.

Jack the Lad

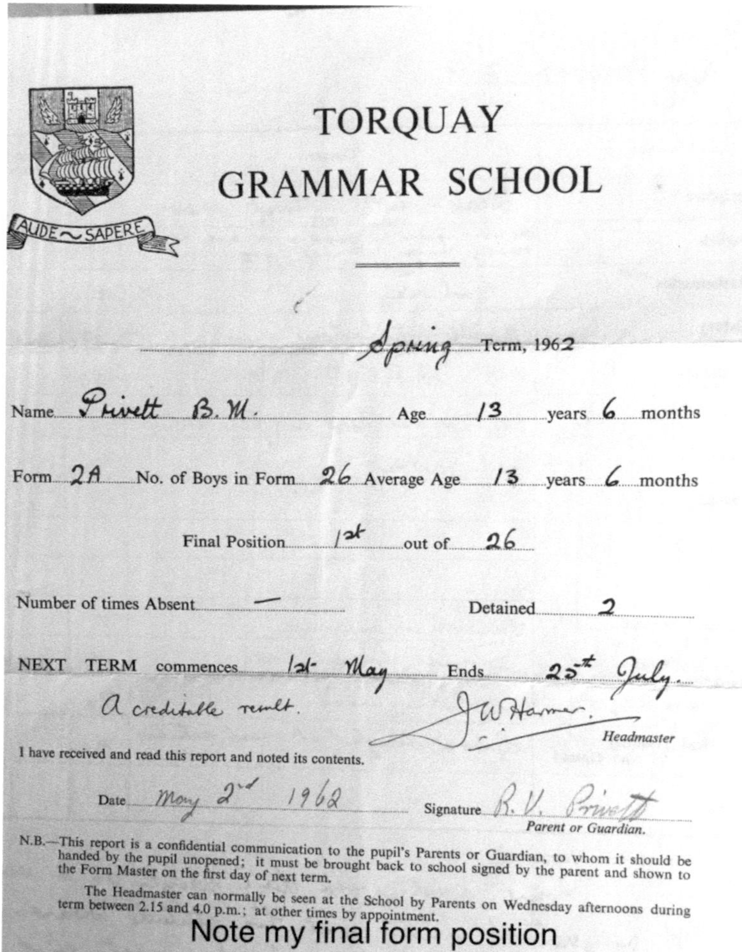

TORQUAY
GRAMMAR SCHOOL

AUDE ~ SAPERE

Spring Term, 1962

Name Privett B.M. Age 13 years 6 months

Form 2A No. of Boys in Form 26 Average Age 13 years 6 months

Final Position 1st out of 26

Number of times Absent — Detained 2

NEXT TERM commences 1st May Ends 25th July.

A creditable result. J W Harmer. Headmaster

I have received and read this report and noted its contents.

Date May 2nd 1962 Signature R.V. Privett Parent or Guardian.

N.B.—This report is a confidential communication to the pupil's Parents or Guardian, to whom it should be handed by the pupil unopened; it must be brought back to school signed by the parent and shown to the Form Master on the first day of next term.

The Headmaster can normally be seen at the School by Parents on Wednesday afternoons during term between 2.15 and 4.0 p.m.; at other times by appointment.

Note my final form position

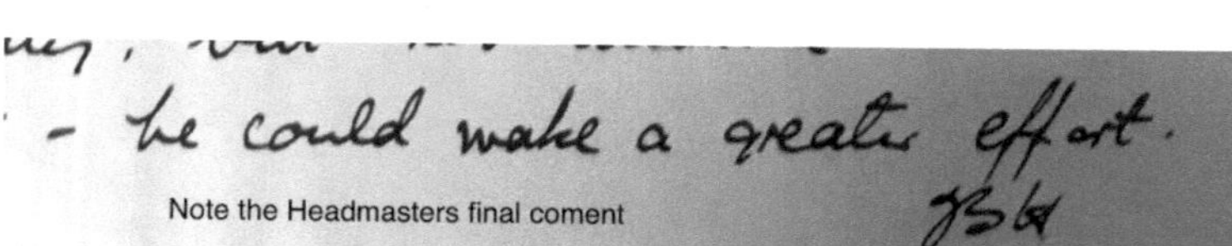

Note the Headmasters final coment

Wish I had this much hair now

I wonder why I shaved the beard off?

Getting married

With my best man Roger

5

A FEW CHANGES

I did apply to be an airline pilot for BOAC and was called for a two-day interview at Hamble near Southampton. The interview included mental arithmetic tests, writing essays, solving mechanical problems and a gruelling two-hour face-to-face interview with one of the most aggressive men I had ever met. For the mental arithmetic test, they put a tape recorder in the middle of the room with a recording of the questions which became harder and quicker, by the time I thought about one question the second one arrived. The essay had to be entitled "Why am I God's gift to BOAC?" Eight people were being interviewed every week for six months and there were only sixteen places, needless to say I didn't get in. I did then consider being a pilot in the RAF but would have to sign on for sixteen years and I decided that was not for me.

At twenty-four years old I got married to Jackie, at the reception which cost £1 per head I forgot I had to make a speech; however, I did succeed using lots of ums and ahhs. The idea was that I would sell my property in Ellacombe Church Road to buy our own place. We found a small plot of land in Kingskerswell, and while looking at it a builder arrived to also look at it, we got talking and agreed if he bought the land and built a bungalow on it we would buy the bungalow. A building society agreed to lend us the money so I didn't have to sell Ellacombe Church Road which was fortunate as I could see a hike in property prices on the way. My stag night was nothing like today's, I just went out with a couple of mates the night before. About 100 people came to the wedding and in the evening, we just went up to Mr Matt's nightclub. The next day we went to stay with my brother for a few days, stopping overnight in a town in East Devon called Beer. With the money we were given at the wedding we bought a fridge and got hold of an old black and white TV but could not afford to put the aerial up so I got an old H-shaped aerial tied it to a broom handle, put it out in the front garden attached to a long aerial lead and turned it round till we got a snowy BBC picture. That was it for many months, the trouble was we had to have the window open to feed the lead through so in the winter it was quite draughty.

Whilst living in Kingskerswell I tried out all three local pubs. One was somewhat rough, one was somewhat cliquey and nobody talked to me, the other was just full of children running around. Driving to Torquay the first pub I passed was called The Devon Dumpling so I called in and was surprised to find I already knew a number of the locals, hence regardless of where I have lived this has been my local for the last 45 years.

Around this time, I decided to grow a beard. After a few months I went to a posh do in my dinner suit and someone said they thought my beard looked scruffy. When I got home after having too many drinks I looked in the mirror and agreed it looked unkempt, so proceeded to tidy it up using scissors. In the morning I found that I had bald patches in my beard so I cut it off leaving just a moustache.

A week or so later I was stopped by the police who said they were looking for men with moustaches to take part in an identity parade. For this I would be paid £1, so I agreed. When I lined up with ten other men, they brought in the suspect who was about six feet tall, blonde but had a moustache. A lady came in and after walking up and down said it was number three, I looked to my left and saw two men making me number three. She left and I asked the police if she had picked me, they said yes but don't worry, then another lady came in who didn't pick anybody. What had happened was that someone had stolen a coat from Marks & Spencer's and these women gave chase to the shoplifter who dropped the coat and escaped. I believe the mistake was the women picked me out because I had played with my group at the Marks & Spencer dinner dance a few weeks earlier and she recognised me from that and not from the shoplifting, however it was a few concerned minutes.

At work, to help make up money me and a work colleague called Bill would volunteer when they were looking for people to help out at other offices. So, we would go to places like Bristol, Southampton, Reading, or London for a week or two at a time and get quite good expenses, as we would share a room and share transport.

Whilst working at the Inland Revenue I used to pay into what we called the 200 club which had a monthly draw of £20 and an annual draw of £500. After not winning a thing for three years surprise surprise I won the £500. I should add as well that I was secretary to our union representative which I seemed to have got badgered into but didn't like doing it.

I used the money I had won in this draw to go to London and buy 500 shirts at a £1 each and I set up a stall at the market selling them for £2 each. I started at Plymouth market on a Saturday and Saltash market on a Sunday. On Saturday I would leave home at 5 am to get a space at the Plymouth market, one day at Saltash market it poured with rain. I only had a trestle table and could not afford a proper stall, so I had to lie over the trestle table on top of the shirts to try and keep them dry and gave a young boy £1 to pull them from under me and put them back in my van.

The problem with the shirts was that the arms were a little narrow and an extremely well-built muscleman bought four shirts and I knew he wouldn't get his arms through, but fortunately he never came back. This wasn't a very fruitful experience as when I bought each box of twenty shirts, they were mixed sizes, and I was always left with the 14 1/2 and 17 1/2-inch collars.

Whilst running my market stall one day I had an experience which made me smile. The man next to me was selling a miracle car cleaner and he had an old car door which was extremely dirty, but when he put the miracle car cleaner on it instantly cleaned the oil and dirt off. However, one day it started to rain, and the rain did a better job of taking off the dirt and oil from his car door than his miracle car cleaner did, so he soon packed up and went home. Another time a gentleman was selling food tins cheap because they didn't have any labels on. He assured people that some had steak and kidney in, some mincemeat and some fruit. However one day a lady brought her tins back and she said she had opened them for her husband's lunch only to find they both had rice pudding in, he apologised and gave her two new tins. He knew that every tin just had rice pudding in, he didn't come back the next week.

After this I went to some auctions to buy up stock from gift shops that had closed and set up a market stall in Kingskerswell, this was a little more profitable but not much.

In 1976 me and Jackie and our friends Norman and Lynn went to America. We each had £200 for a whole month, however we went to Las Vegas where I won a few dollars then off to San Francisco, Los Angeles, San Diego and Tijuana. All this including hiring a car and a helicopter ride through the Grand Canyon for £200 each, although we stayed in some pretty grotty hotels.

Whilst in San Francisco I saw a shop with a queue outside and on checking discovered they were doing old-fashioned photography, dressing people up in yesteryear costumes and had an individual or family photo taken in sepia. Further down the road there was another shop doing the same, so I thought to myself this is for me. Hence the following year I rented a shop in Paignton and set up with the same idea. I don't think Paignton was ready for this, it was three weeks before I took my first photo and I was charging £2.50, (in America they were charging $9.99) so I reduced mine to £1.99. I even had someone come in saying £1.99 it's not even in colour. This was the time of the Wombles so I got a Wombles outfit and me and a friend would take it in turns dressing up in it and going up and down the High Street shouting have your photo taken with Uncle Bulgaria while the other took the photograph for £1. I rented the shop for eighteen weeks and broke even one week and lost on the other seventeen. So, my day consisted of opening up the shop at 8 am, going to work, back at lunchtime so the shop assistant could have a break, coming back at 5 pm till seven, then going off playing keyboard in the evening. At weekends it was the same but instead of my day job I would work the market stall or the photo shop. I used to think if your IQ was less than ten come to Paignton.

During this time, I was still working at the Inland Revenue and playing in my pop group, but it did teach me the rudiments of being an entrepreneur.

Since my early 20s I have always owned a sports car. The first car I bought was a Mitsubishi Starion, I bought it in Plymouth and when I took it down for its first service I asked if they could lend me a courtesy car while it was being serviced to which they agreed. I knew in Plymouth a new supermarket was opening, it was either Asda or Aldi or maybe Lidl's. I thought while I had time on my hands I would go and see what it was all about, so they gave me a little map and off I went. When I got there, I parked in the car park with hundreds of other cars and went in but didn't stay long. When I came out, I realised not only did I not know the make of car they lent me but also, I didn't know its colour, in those days you didn't press a button to open your car you had to use the key. There I was walking up and down through these hundreds of cars looking for mine, the only thing I could remember was that I had left the little map the garage had given me on the passenger seat. What seemed like ages later I found my car with the little map. Luckily, there were no security cameras or else the security guards would have been out in a flash wondering what I was doing.

On mentioning that I have always had a sports car my present one is a Porsche Panamera Hybrid. I had only had it for a few months when driving to work it just died on me and dropped to 5mph I had a line of around twenty cars behind me all doing 5mph. How embarrassing. They eventually replaced the car with another new one.

I came across another property for sale which was a shop with rooms above, but it had been shut down by the council for breaching planning permission rules. It was for sale for £9,500. As the shop was already let all I had to do was convert the upstairs for three young residents who would all have their own bedroom and share a lounge/kitchen and bathroom. I was asking the bank manager to lend me another £8,000 and he thought it was all a good idea, so I asked him for £9,000 instead which he agreed.

Although this was a good investment it was beset with problems. I had squatters in the basement whom the police evicted, I had a blocked sewer and I remember I couldn't go within twenty yards of it because of the smell so I brought in a sewer expert. He was down the hole for ages and shouted up to me, "This is worse than I thought I'm going to have to charge you an extra 50p an hour." The worst problem I had was when someone approached me to rent a small room behind the shop, I initially said no but after him giving me a sob story and saying his council flat would be ready in six weeks I reluctantly agreed. He never paid me a penny although he claimed housing benefit. When he got his housing benefit cheque he would go over to the pub across the road and not come out till all the money had gone. He then moved his girlfriend in and then an Alsatian dog in this 12 x 12 room. After three months I took him to court to have him evicted and the judge accused me of overcrowding!! The judge then asked if I would accept a pound a week off the arrears which I declined and said I wanted him out. The judge then gave him a month to get out. After a month he was still there when I got a call to say he had broken into the flat above to steal any drink he could find, so I had him arrested. I didn't know at the time he already had a string of convictions and the police said he was one of the most violent men in Torquay after he'd been drinking, he was subsequently sent to prison. Would you believe the law said I should keep the room for him till he got out of prison, however I phoned the prison for them to enquire from him where he would like me to take his belongings and they phoned me back with an address. I packed all his stuff up, dropped them on the doorstep of the address, rang the doorbell and walked away. I never heard from him again although I was a little nervous when I found out he had been released.

Oops!

On the Piste

Time for a swim with Norman & Brian Bushel

Glastonbury

6

MORE ON MUSIC

In the group we had differences of opinion of what sort of music we should be playing so in the end decided to call it a day and we split up. One of our final gigs was at an architect's house where we played beside the outdoor swimming pool. The theme for the evening was Vikings and he had fires burning around the pool and everyone was in costume. He had built a bridge over the pool and had jousting competitions until the loser fell into the pool. On one of these challenges someone got his feet caught in the bridge as he fell off and was hanging upside down with his head under water and nobody noticed for some time when he was rescued in a pretty bad state.

My favourite type of music was soul, so we started a new soul band which we called Indiana Highway. The line-up was Dave Klingenberg on drums, Bob Pring on guitar, Dave Mumford bass, myself on keyboard. John Snell on saxophone, Steve Culverhouse on trumpet, and on vocals was Arif Asif. Even though I say it myself it was a very good band, we did a residency for three years from May to September in a night-club on Monday, Tuesday and Wednesday nights. The night-club was called the "Hot Spot" it closed at 2 am but, if you weren't in by midnight the house full sign went up. Once or twice if it was full someone would phone up and say there was a bomb in the place, everyone would be evacuated and then the people who couldn't get in and made the phone call would come in with all the others once the all clear had been given. One evening when we had a bomb scare the police arrived and the sergeant was petrified as he knew nothing about bombs. A mate of mine called Coxy who had been drinking reassured him by telling him he was a bomb disposal expert in the Navy and any problems give him a shout. On this the Sergeant's colour came back to his face and he thanked him. After the all clear the sergeant came over to Coxy and thanked him for his offer to which he replied, "It's a good job you didn't find anything because I couldn't tell the difference between a H bomb and an effing banger" (Coxy in fact was in the Navy but as a diver).

One evening I found Dave our drummer in quite a distressed state and he told me he had just drunk half a bottle of whisky because he was upset that his girlfriend had just left him. That same evening just as we started playing at the nightclub Dave threw up all over his drum kit and consequently we had to stop playing. We were so annoyed that we sacked him, however the next night we reinstated him and just find him £15.

Because I played keyboard, I had developed very strong wrists and fingers and a six foot two bouncer at the nightclub challenged me to grab each other's hand and try and bend them back. This went on for a minute or so till he finally said, "Okay that's enough". I found out the next day I had broken his finger.

Indiana Highway recorded an EP which was like an ordinary vinyl single record except it had two songs on each side and instead of playing at 45 rpm it was played at 33 rpm, the EP stood for extended play. Although it was called "Indiana Highway Live at the Hotspot" it was in fact recorded in a studio and the clapping and cheering between songs was a recording of people at the Albert Hall.

We would play most weekends around Devon and Cornwall and once we were asked if we would be the professional backing group for some singers called the Fantastics. After the Hotspot we were offered six nights a week for six weeks at a holiday camp in Seaton. We didn't realise that this for was for SAGA holidaymakers, many of whom were in wheelchairs and when we played soul music all night for the first night, we were told we wouldn't be required in the future. Our claim to fame though with this band was when we played at Tiffany's nightclub in Exeter. The poster read "Live at Tiffany's nightclub Indiana Highway supported by David Bowie" (this of course was before he became famous). He came on with his acoustic guitar and sang to the audience for half an hour while we had a break. What annoyed me at the time was that he put his cigarette on the top of my Hammond organ and burned a mark on it.

When driving all the way down to west Cornwall we set up and started playing but nobody turned up. After about half an hour the organisers realised, they had forgotten to advertise it so they paid us and we packed up. On the way home we stopped at a club in Plymouth only to find their group hadn't turned up so we set up and played again.

After Indiana Highway I was involved with a few other groups which didn't last very long. Finally we became a trio which was myself on keyboard and doing all the chat, Norman Lindon on sax, flute and vocals and Dave Klingenberg on drums. We did a few summer seasons together then Dave left, and we bought an electric drum machine. One of the first times we used it we were backing a cabaret singer when in the middle of a song he signalled for me to turn up the drums. Not being used to the machine I turned up the speed instead which we thought was very funny, but he did not.

As a duo we once played at Wadebridge County Hall where

they hold the Cornwall County Show. As you can imagine it was huge and when we got there the hall was completely empty except for a stage. We didn't realise that we were playing for the Great Britain Caravan Convention Club and very soon 2,000 people arrived who were staying in their caravans in the area and they all brought their own camping tables and chairs. They asked if we could do some country dancing, so I had to go down and show them while Norman was playing. He said it was quite a sight, about six hundred people on the dance floor with me in the middle showing them what to do.

We stayed together working as a duo for over twenty years, in the end I was doing it for enjoyment and Norman needed the money. We ended up playing in some hotels, if the guests weren't reading the paper, they were looking at me with the expression "Entertain me dare you" so Norman continued on his own.

The Sixth Sense 40 years apart

This group didn't last long

This Group did

This group did

Didn't quite make number one

Me & Norman

They don't make suits like that any more

Mardi Gras

VILA SOL
SPA & GOLF RESORT
ALGARVE · PORTUGAL
Golf in Portugal
DSP

7
CHILDREN, BOATS & SPORT

In 1978 my daughter Leanne was born. The day all my three children were born were the best three days of my life. I remember at her birth I was getting so emotional I was doing all the things the midwife was telling Jackie to do, i.e. deep breathing and pushing. After Leanne was born the midwife seemed to be more concerned about me than Jackie. However, it wasn't as bad as a friend of mine who, when his wife gave birth shouted through his tears, "It's a boy, it's a boy" to which the midwife replied, "No it's a girl, that's the umbilical cord." Stevie Wonder had just released a song called "Isn't she lovely" I went home, put it on and sobbed my heart out. Two years later Daniel arrived, and I went through all the same emotions again.

As I had lived in Torquay all my life, I always fancied having a boat so I bought one. It was a twenty-seven foot Marina with a powerful 50 hp engine. The cost of the boat included a mooring off Shaldon beach, but I don't think I was very popular as the locals didn't like outsiders mooring there. I had a lot of fun with the boat, water skiing, fishing and day trips out, but I wasn't a very good skipper. Once when I was out with my sister and brother-in-law we ran out of petrol and between us had to row back to shore, which took hours. Another time after someone had stolen my tender, I borrowed another tender to get out to my boat but while I was out the person came and took his tender back. When we arrived back we could not get into shore as there was a very strong spring tide and no one would come out to help because the tide was so strong. We had to stay on the boat for many hours.

The worst disaster was after I had taken the boat out for the winter and parked it at Little Oldway. Coxy, Paul and myself then took it down to Paignton harbour and launched it. On our way across the bay, we noticed water in the bottom, but I just assumed it was rainwater. By the time we got to Torquay Harbour it was a foot deep, so me and Paul went back to Paignton to get the trailer to pull it out of the water. When we got back Coxy had gone down and bought a captain's hat and was stood on the deck with water up to his waist saluting and said, "I'm going down with the ship". It transpired that my handyman had not replaced the bung.

Eventually the boat was stolen but was found a month or so later. I claimed off my insurance for the damage and sold the boat without doing the repairs at auction "as seen". In total I just about got my money back.

In sporting challenges, I endeavoured to conquer during the 1970s. Firstly I wanted to complete a marathon, 26 miles 385 yards. I applied to run in the London marathon and was accepted. I would go out training four or five times a week, usually a ten mile run from Kingskerswell to Newton Abbot, along the Newton Road to Torquay, over Torbay hospital and back to Kingskerswell. I marked out the mileposts and each time I went out training I tried to pass each milepost a few seconds quicker. On the day of the marathon, I ran with my brother but partway through lost him in the crowd. At twenty-two miles my calf muscle locked up so for the last four miles I had to jog and walk, hence it took me four and a quarter hours. A few years later I was told that one of my staff at Little

Oldway had terminal cancer and when I went to visit her she told me she had four sons living throughout the UK but could not afford to go and visit them. This was just a few weeks before the Torquay marathon so I thought I would run in it and get sponsored to help her out. I did this and raised £800 which I just put through her letterbox with a note, "Enjoy it. She did as she visited all her sons but sadly two months later died. Because I hadn't trained properly for this marathon it took me weeks to recover from it.

Also in the 70s I took up golf, I went to night school with a friend called Dave to learn the rudiments of golf in the sports hall. We had only been playing a few months when we decided to go to Scotland to play golf. We played at various courses including St Andrews. At St Andrews we had a starter. A queue of people and the people in the restaurant were all watching us as we teed off. We were both very nervous but both hit good shots, I think they were the only good shots we hit all day. The next day we went to Muirfield to watch the Ryder Cup and the first two players we saw, Tony Jacklin and Peter Oosterhuis, we couldn't believe how far they could hit the ball.

After this me and Dave certainly had the golfing bug, we would meet up in Totnes every Sunday morning and drive down to Wrangaton Golf Club where we had both become members. We would play in all weathers, snow, hail, rain, the only trouble was this was a nine-hole golf course with eighteen tees. Because it was on the side of the moors there was a lot of moorland cattle and sheep grazing around the course, at times some of these cows which had huge horns were quite scary. Because of this they put electric fences around the greens to keep the sheep and cattle off, the problem was the top of the electric fence was thirty inches above the ground and my inside leg measurement is only twenty-nine inches. There was a gate to get in, but it always seemed to be on the opposite side to where my ball had landed, on trying to straddle the fence it was often a shocking experience in an unfortunate place. On this course it was the only time I have ever scored a gross seventy-nine. When I left Wrangaton to join Torquay Golf Club my handicap was seventeen, since then it has regularly increased and is now twenty-one and I cannot even play to that.

In 1980 Daniel was born and I was just as emotional as I was with Leanne. Here I was in a secure job which paid well, three properties and a beautiful family. Most people would be content. I wasn't as I hated my job and sometimes I was like a schoolchild thinking what can be wrong with me today. I worked in the Paignton, Torquay and Newton Abbot offices and it was while I was at the Newton Abbot office that I took up squash with a work colleague, Kingsley and eventually joined the squash club and stayed a member for over forty years.

I didn't like the way the Inland Revenue operated. For example, a new inspector went to his neighbour's house for a Residents Association meeting. He was not making notes of the meeting, but valuing his neighbour's carpets curtains and furniture. When he got back to work he looked at his neighbour's file then told another inspector the neighbour shouldn't have been able to afford that furniture, so they should do an investigation on him. Another was someone who had been seen out on his windsurfer, this man ran a small one-man business fitting car exhausts. The inspector checked his file and thought he could not afford the type of windsurfer he was riding. After an investigation, the man could not remember some of the payments. The Revenue classed you as guilty of tax evasion and you had to prove your innocence, even though they could pick on any of the previous six years. As a result, was charged £500 extra tax for the year, but then they said if he had done it for one year he must have done it for six years so that became £3,000. Interest and penalties doubled it, making a total of £6,000. Last I heard of him, he had to sell his business, his wife left him, and he was living in a bedsit.

In fact, years later my file was pulled for an investigation just because an inspector I used to know had seen me driving an old Porsche. Bill, the friend who I used to go on secondment with was still working at the Revenue and phoned me to tell me my file had been pulled. In those days, the Revenue needed two reasons to start a cold investigation and Bill told me one of them was that I had invested more money into Little Oldway, and where did it come from? I was due to send my accounts in for my income from property so immediately sent them in inflating the figures a little higher than I had actually received. I enclosed a letter explaining that I had done better this year with my income from property which allowed me to invest more in Little Oldway. By doing this I had answered their question before they had asked it, so they had to put my file back. Of course, I had to pay a little more tax on my income from property, but this alleviated any time-consuming investigation. Thanks Bill.

I didn't want to be part of this, so I started looking around to set up a business of my own.

8
TIME FOR A CHANGE

I looked at out-of-town restaurants, cut price tyre businesses and many more. Then I decided it was easier to find a property and see what I could do with it, that is when I came across Little Oldway. It was virtually derelict, and the council were considering pulling it down to make a car park, but because it was a listed building there were a lot of objections. I thought it would make an ideal gentleman's club. By that I don't mean a lap dancing club, but a club for gentry with bar, restaurant, snooker room, cigar room and croquet on the lawn. There was a place in London called Churchill's like this which at the time was doing very well (it has since gone bust), however the planners refused it on the grounds of too many cars in and out. Not to deter me I then had the idea of turning it into a care home for the elderly. I must admit I was a little naughty here as at work I started looking through some care home files, and they seemed to be doing quite well. A friend of mine who worked downstairs in the collector of taxes told me that his wife was a matron in a care home called Ardeen Court, but she had left because it was in such a rundown state. He introduced me to her, and she viewed Little Oldway and agreed it would be a good care home, I then brought in CQC (as it is called now) and they agreed. On the strength of this I approached the council who owned it, typical council after a year I still haven't got anywhere so I got some local councillors on my side and finally an agreement was reached. A 99-year lease, £3,500 per year rent and for me to bring the property up to standard, including a new roof within ten years. I took this on without knowing a thing about care homes but felt that I was good at managing people, so I was sure that if I employed people who were experts in the care industry it could work. I asked my friend's wife if when I got it ready would she be the matron, to which she agreed.

The contract was signed on the 6th of February 1982 and I set about completely refurbishing Little Oldway. I had put all my three properties up as collateral to borrow the money from the bank, everyone except two people thought I was mad. The two were Jackie Privett and Brian Bushel who owned a hotel called Carols Court and he had done something similar, to leave a job in London to buy a hotel in Torquay without any knowledge of the hotel trade.

I was now again working every hour of the day playing in my duo two or three nights a week, still working at the Inland Revenue, and working on Little Oldway, though I must admit I did throw a few sickies. I nearly got caught once when a relief inspector stayed in the same hotel I was playing at and reported me, I somehow managed to cover it.

My 70-year-old father helped me with some of the decoration. At one stage he had completely papered the ceiling in the huge lounge before I had got halfway through a small bathroom. However his eyesight was failing a little and after he had emulsioned some of the walls I would go over the bits he had missed after he had gone home.

By July I had completed the lounge, dining room, kitchen and six bedrooms, so I opened. The matron had spoken to some of the old residents at Ardeen Court before she left, who all told her they wanted to move to where she was going to work. So on my opening day, I had six residents from Ardeen Court move in and a month later a seventh all from Ardeen Court. The owner not surprisingly didn't speak to me again for ten years.

I now needed to push on with the refurbishment as seven residents would not cover the wages and upkeep of Little Oldway, hence it was a priority for more bedrooms. As each room was complete I would get a new resident in.

During the alterations me and one of my helpers decided to dress up as a pantomime horse (where I got it from, I've no idea). We pretended to be eating the grass outside the lounge window to the immense amusement of the residents, then we trotted around the side of the house and saw two people walking across the car park. I took off my horse's head and asked if I could help them, they said they were looking for the proprietor as they wanted somewhere for their mother to stay. When I told them I was the proprietor they found it so funny they decided their mother should stay with us and she moved in.

It was now time to resign from the Inland Revenue which I was really looking forward to but with some trepidation, as I would no longer be getting a monthly cheque. With all the office gathered round expecting my speech to be about how I would miss them all, instead I said I had worked in the Revenue for fourteen years and it only seemed like yesterday I joined, and you know what a bloody awful day it was yesterday. Not quite what they expected.

So for the next year Jackie, me and the children had to survive on the money I made playing keyboards which was now five nights per week but not paid very well. One evening after backing a comedian at the Roslyn Hall Hotel Norman, myself, the owner and the barman were having a drink and the

Irish night porter came in as we were discussing the comedian. The owner said, "I think a lot of his jokes went over everybody's head" to which the Irish night porter said “I could hear them alright” needless to say we all burst out laughing.

It wasn't always easy setting up our equipment, my Hammond organ weighed 2 1/2 hundredweight and at one particular working man's club we had to carry it up an outside fire escape. One of my most embarrassing moments was when at the beginning of the season entertainers would all perform in front of hoteliers for them to pick who they wanted in their hotel for the season. On this particular day these were held in a club in Paignton called the Blue Angel. It was now early evening and I asked someone where the gents toilet was. They told me it was down the corridor, first on the right. I went down this corridor and walked in the first door on the right, only to find it a private room with a stag party going on and I walked on the stage just as the stripper was finishing her act. All the men cheered as they thought I was part of the act.

Financially this was a very difficult year, but I soldiered on. The following year got better because the loans I had taken out on the properties had matured so I now received the rent myself and was not paying it to the bank.

By now I was well ahead of my schedule on refurbishing Little Oldway. I did have a lot of trouble with squirrels, I could go into the garden at any one time and see at least ten squirrels. The trouble was they were getting into the building and nibbling through wires. My whole call bell system went down because of this, they also used to eat the plastic dustbins as well as trying to get into the kitchen after the food. I heard one in the attic, I went up with a bit of 2 x 3 in one hand and a torch in the other. A squirrel leapt at me, I took a swing at it and missed. I ran one way he ran the other, I later caught him in the trap.

I phoned the Animal Humane Society to ask what to do

about all these squirrels. They gave me three options. One poison them, two shoot them, three catch them and put them in a sack. I asked what to do when I put them in a sack and they said, "Whack them over the head". I couldn't believe what I was hearing. I couldn't poison them because when I tried it, they would crawl under the floorboards and when they died they made an appalling smell. I couldn't shoot them because there were too many people around, so I bought some traps and caught them live. Now you're not supposed to move squirrels to another area because they are classed as vermin, however I felt I had no option so I would catch them with the help of a resident and set them free, always in the same place in Cockington woods. I would probably remove five or six per week for many weeks. A couple of months later there was an article in the evening paper saying that the council were going to have to do a cull on the squirrels as there was so many of them in Cockington woods.

By now I was getting used to elderly people, in fact every Saturday morning I would go to speak to every resident and do their shopping. I had one resident who was put on a diet by her doctor, so for lunch she had a Ryvita and salad. When she had finished, she said “I’ve eaten my diet can I have my lunch now”. Of course we gave her a proper lunch. Another two amusing but sad cases. Firstly a married couple who shared a room, sadly during the night the husband died next to her. When she was told in the morning her reply was “Oh dear, what’s for breakfast?” Secondly twin sisters who had never been married and lived together all their lives. When one died her sister would not accept it, so we took her to the chapel of rest to see her. When we took her in, and her sister was lying there all she said was “Nice carpet”.

I now I had eighteen residents at Little Oldway and felt I should do my bit for charity. Every year for sixteen years I held a garden fete where I would invite all the local charities to have a stall and they could keep what they took. I would charge a small entrance fee and put on a coconut shy, a bric-a-brac stall and a tea garden. I would also put on entertainment, like dancers, jugglers and singers throughout the afternoon. The night before the first garden fete I had a dream that only one bald headed man would turn up. I told my matron this and fifteen minutes before we were due to open, she took me round to the front of the building. The queue to get in was over fifty yards long.

To start with I got minor celebrities to open it but as it became more and more popular, I got more famous celebrities. The first of whom was Norman Wisdom who was one of my favourites when I was a child, and he didn't disappoint. He was the first to suggest as I walked around with him that I should carry a bucket to collect donations when people asked for his autograph or a photo with him. I did this on all subsequent garden fetes. I also had Michael Barrymore, Jimmy Cricket, John Inman, Danny La Rue, Joe Pasquale, Bernie Winters and Les Dawson. When Les Dawson came, he said he could only stay for twenty minutes as he had a commitment, I knew what he meant, he thought we would just give him a cup of tea and talk about old people. However, I always did my homework to find out what they drank and after talking about golf and ten cigarettes and him having umpteen gin and tonics he was taken home three hours later. He had only just got married and I had to laugh at an article written by his new wife in the News of the World colour supplement stating how she had changed Les who no longer smoked or drank. Les was my favourite of all the celebrities. As I said I did my homework and I discovered Danny La Rue liked a special type of champagne. I tried everywhere to get it and finally had to make a special order. When he came, I brought him a glass, and he said "No thanks I'll just have a tonic water". Bernie Winters was just the opposite, he arrived late, didn't know what to do, wouldn't circulate amongst the public, and on leaving someone asked for a photograph, to which his wife said “come on

Bernie we haven't got time for that". Not my favourite celebrity.

I also put on a charity golf day for many years where I invited suppliers to enter a three-man team. I called this the Little Oldway Golf Challenge Trophy and each year thirty to forty people entered. We raised considerable money for various charities, although my team never won.

Living out in Kingskerswell, when I drove home from a gig late at night on occasion I would come across farm animals which had escaped. Once a whole herd of cows, once a flock of sheep who took over my front garden and also a very large goose in the back garden, on another occasion the whole lane was blocked by horses.

I had put a small extension on the bungalow but as I was now feeling a little more secure financially I thought it would be better to move nearer to Little Oldway. I hated the country lane from Kingskerswell to Torquay, I had some very near misses and some scrapes. I did once come round a blind corner and went straight into a ten-ton lorry which was blocking the road. Although I was not hurt my car was extensively damaged. Another time a car was coming so fast it ripped my wing mirrors off and scraped the side of my car. The lady driver stopped for a second then drove off, I managed to get the number plate and reported it to the police. I was asked to produce my licence etc which I took back later. They then told me the woman driver denied it and she had so many dents and scratches on the car there was nothing they could do. A few days later I got a warning letter from the police stating that I should have taken my documents in within seven days and I took nine days. Doesn't give you much faith in the police.

Never doing things in a conventional manner, I found a plot of land coming up for auction in Monterey Close. I found there was not a lot of interest in it as it was thought there was an underground stream running through it. I did some research and found that the builder who had built the small estate had been refused planning permission to put two houses on the site. They lost their appeal and could only build one house, and although there was no size restriction by then they had taken all their machinery back to Cornwall. I had tests done on the ground and there was no underground stream.

The expected price for the plot was £40,000. Prior to the auction I offered £36,000 which was refused. I knew there wasn't a lot of interest in the auction as they phoned me up to see if I was going. I was very coy and told them I'd go if I had time because I'd seen another plot which wasn't in fact true. Anyway I went to the auction and got the plot for £35,000. £1,000 less than my original offer. Then with the help of an architect I went about designing the new house. The result was a very futuristic design which was turned down by the planners because they said it was not in keeping with the other houses in the area, but I was told I would get permission if I appealed. As this would take twelve months the design was altered to a more conventional house which was passed, although a neighbour across the road put in an objection which read "I must appeal in the strongest possible terms about that Dallas type of building being built opposite". When the build started, I put up a sign, Southfork which was the name of the house in the TV series. The neighbour didn't share my sense of humour and it was many years before he spoke to me.

Kingskerswell was sold and we spent many months staying in friends' houses or one of my one-bedroom flats. Four of us in one bedroom was not the most comfortable time. I had many an argument with the builder as I went up there every day to see how things were progressing. At one time I asked him to put one line of soldier course bricks, which means they lay the bricks vertically not horizontally. While I was talking with the builder his bricklayer did this which took him probably half an hour. He charged me some exorbitant fee for this, and we totally fell out and he walked off site but did come back later. So, the house was called Monterey House, we moved in only to find Jackie was expecting our third child and a few months later Ben was born. I was still just a wreck at his birth.

I did make one mistake regarding the house. I was one of the first in the area to have automatic electric doors on my garage. When they were fitted the engineer forgot to tell me to put my own code in the remote as they were on factory settings. A neighbour was so impressed with these doors, he ordered the same but also did not change the code. We were away on holiday when he had his fitted and so every time he opened his garage door mine opened as well. At this time, I had a particularly good community bobby called Neil and he sorted it all out before my return.

My next project was to extend Little Oldway. To finance this I sold the shop and flat in Torre at a good profit and used the money to pay for this extension.

In order to do this extension, I had to demolish some outbuildings, the problem was it is a grade two listed building and planning permission took forever. Applying to the council to increase the number of residents to over twenty-five was a nightmare. After eighteen months work started, it took about a year with me, a site foreman named Coxy, and subcontractors to do various tasks. I did save a lot of money by setting up my own business which I called Torre Construction and because I was altering a grade two listed building the company which I owned got the VAT back. The VAT inspector said what I had done was very clever but totally legal.

Just before this a few of my friends had bought deluxe caravans and I bought a little four berth caravan for £200, then on our first trip I let all the children paint it with flowers etc. I used this caravan as a site hut for the building work and after all my friends had sold their caravans each at an enormous loss, I had a carpet layer who quoted me £300 to lay all the carpets in the extension. During a conversation he told me he was looking for a little caravan, hence we did a deal. He had by now a very dirty and muddy caravan and I had the carpets laid for free. All sixteen new rooms were purpose built, and all had en-suite facilities. I also had a lift installed, an office, laundry room and sun lounge. Despite everyone's initial reservations Little Oldway was doing very well with twenty-eight residents and my original matron stayed with me for sixteen years.

EVERY YEAR A BUNCH OF US WENT TO WATCH THE ONE-DAY cricket tests. One time we could not get tickets for the one-day so went to Lords Cricket Ground to see Dickie Bird's last test match as an umpire. I had got hold of a life-size cut out of Dickie Bird and when he gave the first person out, I stood it up on the seat. Everyone around was laughing until the steward came and told me to take it down. I told him we were only having a bit of fun. I remember distinctly his reply, "you're not here to have fun you're here to watch the cricket". Pompous Lords. Originally it was my job to provide lunch for everyone and I would go to town with smoked salmon, duck rolls, strawberries and cream, etc. One day when I was leaving to pick everyone up, I had left the basket of food behind the vehicle. I forgot and ran it over crushing everything. Another time we came across two young men who had been given too much change for their ticket purchase and spent it all on beer, by lunchtime they were plastered and kept threatening to do a streak. We persuaded them to wait till the end, and near the end they went down to the boardings just wearing a t-shirt and nothing else. A policeman came over and instead of arresting them asked them to move behind the boardings which caused much hilarity from the crowd. Of course they did streak at the end and I don't know what happened to them.

Twice I dressed up in a very authentic gorilla suit. The first time was when an old colleague of mine was retiring from the Inland Revenue and he was the last joker there. Even though I had left some years before someone phoned me and asked if I could do a prank, so just as he started his final speech which he was extremely nervous about doing, the person phoned me. I burst into the office in the gorilla outfit, picked him up and carted him off. After smothering his face with lipstick, I dumped him back outside the office. Almost half an hour later I walked in, as he had invited me to his leaving do, I apologised for being late and he said, "You'll never guess what happened to me half an hour ago." To the day he died he never knew it was me.

The second time was for my then sister-in-law's birthday. She lived in Wokingham and they were having a party. Dressed as a gorilla I rang the doorbell. She answered it and I picked her up and ran down the road with her on my shoulder screaming, I hadn't thought this one through too well and after a hundred yards I wondered what to do so I just put her down and walked away. When I later walked into the party, she knew immediately it was me as I was the only one of my family missing. I remember going to Wembley to watch Torquay United in a promotion play-off against Bournemouth. It went to extra time and Torquay won on penalties. My brother was having a birthday party in Wokingham that night and because of the football we were late which didn't go down too well.

On a serious issue one evening during my meal at home I suddenly keeled over in pain. I was taken straight down to the doctors who fortunately had a late-night surgery, who in turn sent me straight to hospital. By late that night I was being operated on, in the morning the surgeon came round and told me it was a major swelling of the bowel and he didn't know what caused it but he had taken out my appendix and told me I was all clear. He then went to the next bed to me where a man maybe a year or two older than me lay, I was about thirty at the time. He told him he had a major swelling of the bowel, but this was caused by a severe inoperable cancer and there was nothing they could do for him. Did I thank God that night.

One thing I have found is that I hate it when Big Brother tries to bully me. When I first took a mortgage out with Halifax, because of the amount they were offering, 0.5% less as long as the market forces allowed. About five years later by chance I saw a statement showing 0.2% less. After making enquiries they said they had advertised it and I said that was not good enough, the contract had said they should inform me directly. When they said they had, I asked for a copy of the letter they had sent me. They sent me a letter which they said was similar to the one they sent me. I said this wasn't good enough and if they couldn't show me the exact copy of the letter, I would sue them. I got a letter back saying they were sorry and would credit me with the difference in the percentage which was about £2,000. Another time my matron and I went to visit a resident who had been in hospital for some time. The patient was having a bed bath at the time, so I didn't go in, but my matron did. My resident had been in hospital for a month and the staff nurse told her that she had bedsores, implying that we had caused them. For those who don't know the bedsore can arrive overnight and she had been in hospital for a month, so my matron took this up with the ward sister. When we made the complaint, we were told the ward sisters report included "Mr Privett stormed out in a huff". I took exception to this as I had not even been in. Because of the bedsores the ward sister was trying to cover her back. I demanded an apology. I told my solicitor, saying I only wanted an apology and acknowledgement that the bedsores were caused by the hospital. He told me I wouldn't get one as the ward sister would probably lose her job, but I received £5,000 in compensation.

Over the years I have had a habit of putting my foot in it so much that the staff now refer to these as Barryisms. Here are a few examples. On the 5th of November, a lady resident was getting into the lift at work, and I said to her, "Aren't you going to stay and watch the fireworks?" forgetting that she was totally blind. Once there was a noise outside the office and I jokingly shouted, "What has happened, has someone's leg fallen off?" and of course the noise was made by a man with only one leg. That Christmas I was doing the Christmas draw and the next prize was a very little bottle of body lotion, I said "You'll need to have a very small body for this", a thirty-eight stone lady won it. Another time a resident asked for a load of loose change and I said, "Once all this is in your pocket you will walk with a limp", this man had had a stroke and already walked with a pronounced limp. Doing one of my magic tricks I told a resident to pick a card, look at it, show everyone else what it is, remember it and put it back in the pack. I had forgotten that this man was totally blind.

I felt I needed another project, so I bought a property at the right price and converted it into two flats which has proved to be a good investment.

Sadly, by now I felt things were not right at home and I do not intend going into details of the reasons, but I moved out. I had met my current partner Jacky but still finished up living alone with no partner for six months. This was a very dark time for me. However, I have always had great support from all my family, my sisters Julie and Dawn, my brother Roger and although my parents were not aware for some considerable time, I always had their full support. I feel that I am blessed with a remarkably close family but not very close to the others, like auntie's uncles, cousins etc. My grandmother lived to be 101 and in honour of her hundredth birthday a garden party was arranged, and cousins spent the afternoon introducing themselves to each other. I once passed a man in the street and we both nodded as though we knew each other, and it wasn't till later I realised it was my uncle, although by then he had separated from my aunt.

I only met one of my father's brothers or sisters and we

were quite excited when she came to visit us. She was very wealthy, she owned a string of houses and a petrol station in Cheltenham. She told my father she had made her will to leave the majority of her wealth to her doctor and solicitor, however she was going to take care of her family soon. A short time later the envelope arrived and with bated breath my father opened it to find a cheque for £50.

My grandmother had ten children from her two husbands although we are sure nine were from her two husbands and one from A.N. Other. Her first husband had died before I was born but I remember her second husband, Bert had enormous ears but was virtually deaf. All my uncles died before they reached seventy years old except the one from A.N. Other who at the time of writing this is still alive, but I haven't seen him in years.

I was now moving from flat to flat, the first one I had was in the block next to the Corbyn head hotel, called Corbyn Suites. As they were short term holiday flats I asked the owner if I rented it for two months would I get a discount. He said he couldn't as he was only supposed to let for holiday use but if I stayed for two months, he would only charge me for the basic one-bedroom flat but upgrade me to the best available at no extra charge. For six of the eight weeks I stayed in the three-bedroom penthouse which was very luxurious.

Sadly, over the next couple of years I lost three dear friends, all of whom were in their early fifties. There was a story attached to each of these friends.

Firstly, Dave Hyne. We went to France with four other friends and when we got off the ferry, we decided to have a kitty to which he replied, "After I bought a drink and a meal on the ferry I haven't any money left." We also all had to take a trophy and he didn't, so we called his the invisible trophy. On that same trip we all went on a bender drinking Calvados apple brandy. The next morning someone suggested having a glass of fresh apple juice, which just put us back into the condition we were in the night before. When we played golf Dave went first and was hitting his fifth shot and still hadn't reached the ladies tee. Another time someone we both knew had had a very expensive tie bought for him by his wife for his birthday, but Dave didn't like it so he just cut it off with some scissors. The mutual friend went back to get a replacement only to find they were one-offs so he couldn't get a replacement. I have no idea what his wife said. We put up with all Dave's shenanigans because he was such a likeable character.

Next Jeff White, whom I went to London with to watch Bruno in a boxing tournament. Afterwards we roomed together in a very large room with single beds on opposite walls. Despite this he still managed to wake me up in the morning with the loudest fart I have ever heard. When he died there were about 300 mourners at his funeral and as we came out and signed the book of remembrance "True love ways" by Buddy Holly was being played. As there were so many people this song was on a loop and played over and over again. A week or so later the landlord of my pub, who had been to the funeral, put Buddy Holly's greatest hits on his pub CD but when it got to "True love ways" it ejected. Scary.

Bill Loram was buried the same day as Princess Di, at 9 am in Brixham. I had had a late night before and didn't wake up till 8:30 so missed it, something I have always really regretted. Bill had been the man I had shared with when I worked at the Inland Revenue. We went on secondment to other towns together and shared a room, he still worked there and was the one who tipped me off when my file had been pulled, thus avoiding an investigation. I had only spoken to him six weeks before, when he told me he was suffering with bad headaches. He was diagnosed with a brain tumour and passed away very quickly. A great sportsman, he played football to a high standard and at the time of his death trained athletes in Brixham.

I don't know where I found the time but I wrote, produced and acted in a pantomime. It was called Cinderfella, an adults only pantomime. Instead of Cinderfella losing a slipper she lost a giant condom. There were only five people in it and Cinderfella was played by a man who pretended to be very camp. Although I say it myself it was hilarious, I was a pregnant ugly sister. We did a one night only show to a sell-out audience The headmaster of the boys grammar school let us use their school hall and we raised over £800 which was sent to the children in need charity.

After moving out of the Corbyn Suites I spent the next eighteen months moving from flat to flat, six months in each flat, until I saw a new development being built in Marldon and reserved one of the houses.

At this time Little Oldway was running so smoothly I felt I needed something more to light my fire. My first thought was to open a health farm mainly for ladies, with the idea that ladies from all over the UK could come down for a week or so of pampering. If their husbands came as well and they didn't want the pampering I would arrange for them to have a golfing holiday. I found two properties which I felt were suitable and made a sealed bid for one of them. There were ten bids and when they were opened one was extremely low, seven, including mine were very close to each other and two others were over twice what everyone else was bidding. I did not understand the logic of this, however one of these two was accepted. The other place I looked at was in West Ogwell and was occupied by nuns. There were forty small bedrooms and in the grounds was a church and a cemetery. I did some redesigning of the layout which involved the church being turned into an indoor swimming pool. I then found out they wanted to keep it within the ecclesiastical jurisdiction, and it was sold to some religious organisation.

My next idea was to go into the licensing trade. The landlord of my local pub was in financial difficulties and I got close to buying my local pub, but he pulled out at the last moment. After this I visited quite a few pubs and in fact made an offer for one in Newton Abbot that didn't sell any food whatsoever but had a large room joining onto the pub which could easily be turned into a restaurant. However, this was bought by someone else very quickly and I notice that now that large room is a restaurant. Then someone said to me, "Barry why don't you stick to what you're good at" i.e. the care industry and I thought to myself, "He's right."

9

SAFARI

One thing I have always been keen on is wild animals, especially big game. I was reading an article in the paper written by a hunter turned game guide who said he had found an ideal spot in Zambia to build a safari camp and was looking for a sponsor. I was intrigued and got in touch with him to find he lived quite close. After meeting him a few times he went back to Zambia and I said I would think about it. A few weeks later I was on a plane heading for Zambia. From Lusaka which is the capital it took two days to get to the South Luangwa Valley where he had suggested the Safari camp was to be built. I was being driven in a jeep with a driver, a guard and the ex-hunter. The last six hours was over a mountain with a very narrow track which was breaking away and sometimes the vehicle was at an angle of 30° towards a drop to infinity. It didn't help that the driver kept telling me where vehicles had gone over including one place, he said "A vehicle went over here and they never found the bodies". We eventually got to the site and they pitched up a tent for me in the deep bush. I got very little sleep that night, all I could hear were the animals calling, although I had a guard with a gun outside my tent all night. I showered in the morning with a bucket of cold water dripping drops till it tilted and the water poured over me. After my shower four or five natives just wearing loincloths came out of the bush and stood about ten yards away just staring at me, I think I was probably the first white man they had seen. One was smoking a rolled-up newspaper, I noticed that another of them had a festering wound on his shin so I beckoned him over and put ointment and a bandage on his wound. He left to go back to his mud hut which was probably a mile away and brought me back an ear of corn as a thank you.

Next thing I knew was the native whose leg I had bandaged turned up with a dugout canoe to take me fishing. His canoe leaked like a sieve, so we stopped in some bulrushes to bail it out. I asked the native, who spoke very broken English, if there were any crocodiles to which he replied with a big smile on his face, "Oh yes Massa loads". I have never bailed out so quickly in my life. Anyway I surveyed the whole area and explained to the ex-hunter that while it was a good spot the infrastructure was impossible not only to get the track through but the river nearly always flooded during the rainy season and people would be unable to cross it.

Before I left the natives gave me a plant as a gift, I was pretty sure it was a marijuana plant, so I thanked them and left it on the floor of my tent ready to throw away after they left. Later, after I had packed up my tent and was on my way back, I suddenly realised I had not taken the plant out of my tent. I opened it but could not find it. You can imagine my concern when I came back to the UK and had to go through customs and sniffer dogs, but it was all clear and I still don't know what happened to the plant.

The next night was spent with a missionary, one of the few people in my life I have been in awe of. He didn't get back till late, maybe around midnight after he had just driven over the same mountain we had on his own. He did this once a week and every year he would just go off into the bush with a gun for up to two months to go and see his people. A nun who also worked there cooked me a meal in the evening. When I asked her what it was, she said Impala and when I asked her where she got it from, she replied that she had shot it herself that morning. After dinner me and the missionary sat up under what must have been a million stars talking. I had heard he liked his whisky, so I brought a bottle for him we went to bed at about five o'clock in the morning. By seven o'clock I could hear his voice outside talking to the people who had come to his little chapel and there he was taking a service. What a man.

During the evening I kept hearing the noise of a moped, so in the morning I enquired what it was for. The nun told me that there was a six bed hospital about a mile away which she looked after. It was the only hospital within thirty miles and a lady was very poorly there, so she went down every hour or so to check on her. I asked her why she didn't stay there to which she replied that there were no extra beds. On our return back a few days later I got the driver to do a detour back to see her as I had a camp bed. When I gave it to her it was though I had given her the crown jewels, she couldn't thank me enough.

Another scary incident I had on this trip was on a dark night when I was taken out on a safari. It was just me with a driver and a guard in an open jeep, no roof, no doors and I sat in the back on an elevated seat. We came across six lions hunting a herd of Impala. Two of the lions were parallel with the Jeep, one about twenty feet away, another two were coming in on a 45° angle from the west and two male lions were just lying down behind us. Now there was a rule that you don't shine your spotlight at the lions because the Impala will see them and you don't shine the torch at the Impala because it will dazzle them, you shine it up in the air, so you just see an outline of the lions. We spent about forty minutes moving very slowly, as the lions moved, we moved, and we were only about eighty yards from the Impala when the lion which was only twenty feet away from me went missing. You can now imagine here I am sat on a very high seat alone in the back of a jeep in the dead of night with six lions around me, one of which I could not see. This went on for about five or ten minutes although it seemed more like five or ten hours, till something spooked the Impalas and they all ran off with the lions in pursuit. The worst thing I saw was a buffalo stuck in the mud and the crocodiles were eating it from underneath while the lions were around waiting their turn.

I couldn't get over how poor the people were, whole families sometimes three generations would just live in a mud hut. They would sit outside where they did the cooking and sleep in the hut and the bushes were their toilet. No electricity, no running water. Every village I went to seemed to have one child who was blind, it was called river blindness, caused by a fly laying their eggs in their eye. An antidote would cost 50p, but the families couldn't afford it. If a village had an ox, they were treated like hierarchy and a few villages had wells which were built by a water charity. When we were coming across the mountain earlier, we came across three people walking over the mountain with produce they were delivering on their heads, it took them twenty-four hours to walk over the mountain for which they were all just given a square meal.

During this trip I came across the worst road accident I have ever seen. A petrol tanker and trailer had overturned and crushed several cars, spilling its contents down the road. We were the third car at the scene but when we saw someone walking through the accident smoking my driver, who was a special constable shouted, “Let’s get out of here.” I read in the paper later that there were multiple deaths.

The last night I stayed in a hotel at the top of Victoria Falls. Security guards walked around with catapults which they used to scare off the monkeys. My guard wanted to sleep in the Jeep but security would not allow him to so he slept on the balcony. The evening meal was a buffet type but my guard didn't recognise any of the food so I plated him up some fish and chips. He wouldn't sit on the same table as me, so I sent him somewhere else. Then I realised he had never used a knife and fork before, so I taught him. In the morning it was a buffet breakfast, so I just gave him a croissant and jam and then spotted him trying to eat it with a knife and fork. Before I left, he took me round to meet his family in his mud hut. His wife came out with two children, one she was carrying had runny eyes and nose. I asked if she had a cold and she replied, "No she has malaria".

ALTHOUGH I WAS UNSUCCESSFUL REGARDING THIS SAFARI camp I did like the idea and so a few months later went back again, this time with a friend of mine Tony to look at various safari camps which were for sale. On our two-day drive to South Luangwa Valley we stopped at the only hotel en route. I say hotel, but it was virtually a derelict building. The bath was all stained and had insects in it and just a trickle of cold water. The owner said there was a shower block outside. Tony went to investigate and returned saying, "We'll use the bath." The owner then asked us if we would like a meal and on asking him what he had he told us he had chicken or chips or chicken and chips. We had our meal with praying mantises on the table and wall.

During this trip we went white water rafting, starting from the bottom of the Victoria Falls, spending all day rafting down the Zambezi River. There were six of us in the raft plus a guide and it was a lot more treacherous than I expected. In the first couple of hours three of the people in the raft had been thrown out and we had to pull them back in with cuts and bruises on them, at one stage the guide said, "If you fall out here swim to the right, because on the left it is called the washing machine and if you get caught in it you will just be spun underneath the water." When we got to rapid eighteen the guide said, "Do you want to go down the hard route or the very hard route?" Being very bolshie we all agreed to go down the very hard route. What our guide should have said was, "Do you want to go down the extremely hard route or the impossible route?" because when we went down the raft was thrown ten feet into the air and we were all thrown out. Although I had a life jacket on, I was still under water for some considerable time and about ten minutes later I was dragged out of the water semi-conscious. Since that date I cannot go into water out of my depth. I found out later that a total of three people had died on that river during the year.

While there we went on a number of safaris and also viewed safari camps that were for sale, but none were suitable.

As we couldn't get a flight back to the Lusaka me and Tony had to hire a private plane but the pilot was so cocky when I asked him would be this plane be able to glide if the single engine cut out. He replied that it would glide like a stone which put the fear of Christ into us.

However just before we left, I was shown a safari camp called Chinchilli Lodge which had been built for the country's president, but he never used it and it had fallen into disrepair. I didn't have much time to inspect it so a few months later I went back to Zambia again, this time with Tony and another friend Coxy. We stayed at Chinchilli Lodge and went on various safaris and even another white water raft but this time as the water was a lot deeper it wasn't so scary. I was quite impressed with the safari camp and worked out what I could do with it and the alterations and costs which would have to be made. When I got back to home, I made an offer for the safari camp but was beaten to it by a company from South Africa.

Every time I went back to Zambia, I would take two full suitcases full of clothes, toys, pencils and colouring books and when I went around to the villages, I would ask the village elder if I could distribute them to his people. Distributing to the children first, then the ladies, then the men, but I would always keep back one of those old-fashioned dinner shirts with frills down the front for the village elder. One of the villages invited me back for a meal of cooked roots and while I was there a man who was well over six feet tall came out wearing a bright yellow pair of my old golfing trousers, they barely covered his knees.

By now I had conceded that I was not going to be the proprietor of a safari camp.

10
BUILDING THE EMPIRE

Let's go back to the statement, stick to what you're good at. My chemist had told me months previously that Ardeen Court (the home that my first residents for Little Oldway came from) was up for sale. I looked up the details only to find he was asking a crazy price for it. Later the agent told me that because they were in serious financial trouble the bank told them they had to reduce the price by 50%. On the strength of that I was a little more interested and arranged a viewing. I had never been in such a disgusting place, there were forty bedrooms each one no more than ten feet by ten feet, only three bathrooms and four toilets in the whole place. The mattresses had the stuffing coming out of them, curtains falling down and very little floor covering, and the smell, well I got part way down the ground floor hallway and couldn't go any further because of the smell. They told me there were eleven residents, but I found out later that three of them were on respite and would be leaving at the end of the month. After coming out the agent asked what I thought, and I told him in my opinion it was only worth 50% of the new asking price which of course was 25% of the original asking price. The agent laughed, told me I must be joking and left. About two months later the agent phoned me and said that whilst it was a laughable offer it was the only offer they had received, and the bank was about to foreclose. They asked if I could increase my offer and I said If they included the old minibus and the phone system which belonged to his secretarial company, I would increase by £5,000. A few days later they came back and accepted it.

What a job I had taken on—I now had eight residents but a lot more staff. During the next eighteen months I would not allow anybody except the residents' visitors to come into the home as I was too embarrassed to own a care home in such dreadful condition. The previous owner had all the staff doing all the jobs. They took it in turns fetching day patients, cooking the tea, cleaning and making the beds, and also doing a meals on wheels service. I called all the staff in to introduce myself and told them I would not be like a bull in a china shop, but within twelve months they would notice a lot of changes. The care manager was left to do everything unchecked, she lived along with her husband and two children in a small flat at Oldway Heights. Her husband was the handyman, and he was the first to go, I found he spent all his time in his workshop making things for himself, including a wooden canoe. I banned him from his workshop, which he was quite upset about. Then I found out his wife, who was doing the wages, had paid him for ninety-nine hours in one week, so she went as well. All done, within twelve months over 50% of the staff had left, I think it was because they were not used to doing a day's work. The remaining staff were quite excited at the way things were turning out.

I couldn't afford to bring in a builder to do all the alterations, so I had to oversee all the alterations myself and brought in a plumber, electrician and carpenter, the rest was done by me and some labourers. The carpenter was a real joker. He once put a towel rail on the wall and I told him it wasn't straight. He immediately replied that it was an automatic towel rail, you put the towel on at the far end and by the time you had washed your hands the towel had slid down the rail towards you to dry your hands. I had many a laugh with him.

Slowly but surely the place started to take shape. The old floor was in some places partly covered with Flowtex and I wanted some for a small toilet but couldn't find a piece big enough in the whole building to use. I enlarged all the rooms and gave every one of them en-suite facilities.

Over the first six years of owning Oldway Heights I had several managers who didn't work out too well, but then had a very good care manager who loved animals. She had a whippet which followed her around, and she kept ferrets and guinea pigs although the ferret got out and killed all the guinea pigs. On one occasion when I came back from holiday, she told me we had two new residents then took me out the back to see she had bought two goats and had built a shelter and electric fence around their running area. Even with the electric fence they kept escaping. Unfortunately, a few years later she pressed me to give the staff a substantial pay rise and I explained I could only do this if I increased the fees to cover it. I did all the sums and gave her all the details of the new fees and as promised I did the pay rise. It wasn't until a few months later I noticed one of the resident's fees wasn't as much as I had calculated so I checked the others and likewise they were lower. When I confronted my care manager about this, she said that she felt I had put the fees up too much so she reduced my figure. As you can imagine a row broke out and things were never the same. She left not long after taking the goats with her. However, for the last fifteen years I have had the same manager who ticks all the boxes.

The first few years of running Oldway Heights was so difficult, while I was dating Jacky, I was living from flat to flat with none of them being particularly nice. I was again putting in fourteen hour days but losing money hand over fist. In year two/three I made a loss of £35,000 and it was almost an enjoyment at the end of the month of hundreds of hours work, a year later to find out I had only lost £1,000 which I classed as a result. Still, I soldiered on as I had done my research and was sure there was an opening for a home for the younger physically handicapped. It seems a shame that someone in their fifties/sixties who had an injury, early Parkinson's, a stroke or other debilitating disabilities should be put in an old people's home where average age was eighty-five. Similarly, you get people who are seventy-five coming on sixty who don't want to go into an old people's home. The only other place similar was Leonard Cheshire home in Brixham, but we prided ourselves as being more like a home from home, where they were more like a hospital. It was a long time before social services accepted that what we were doing was just as good and we found that social services started to give preference to Oldway Heights.

Now I noticed a new housing development being built in Marldon and put a deposit on one which they hadn't started building yet. When it was finished I noticed it didn't have a full-size chimney on it although it didn't worry me. Not to miss a trick, I said it spoilt the overall look, as a result of this I had the house completely carpeted and a six range cooker, which was the same as the one in the show home, I also had the master bedroom knocked through to the fourth bedroom to make a large dressing room. All this for free in place of a chimney. After six to eight months it was finished, and I moved in and thoroughly enjoyed living there. We had a residents association of which I joined the committee and we put on events in the adjoining field. When they built the house next door they encroached on my garden with a drive-by about two feet and as a result of this had a dividing wall built and the garden laid out again for free.

Somehow, I still found time to have a social life still playing squash, when four of us every week would have a round robin tournament. One of the four later went to work in Africa and was the only person I ever knew who died of Aids. Twice I went on squash tours with the club, once around Cornwall and once to the Channel Islands. It was during the Cornish trip that in an attempt to get to the ball I ran into the squash court wall and was knocked unconscious. Still to this day if I touch the side of my head, I get pins and needles through the back of my eyes.

John & Sally

Jim &Val

Rob&Coxy

Tony

The ladies

A formal photo of friends

Not so formal

Kay and Rob

Little Oldway

Oldway Heights

11
LONG WEEKENDS AWAY

Every year I would organise a weekend trip for the lads at the Devon Dumpling, usually within two hours of home. The landlord never came with us but always gave me a few pounds to buy the lads a drink. I personally knew Jethro the comedian and found he was doing a show nearby, so I persuaded him to come over to our hotel when he had finished at the theatre and give us a private show. I used the money the landlord had given me to pay him although it wasn't much. It was a great night with Jethro doing jokes by request. My favourite was, "My wife is so ugly when we got married the vicar said to me will you take this woman to be your wedded wife and I said I do, and he looked back at her and said to me I'm going to ask you again."

On another occasion in Newquay one of our party, Bob damaged his Achilles tendon whilst playing tenpin bowling and couldn't bear any weight whatsoever, so we got hold of an old decrepit wheelchair with small wheels. We brought him into town, bought him a penny whistle, put a hat in front of him and a sign saying please give generously and left him in the High Street while we all went down the pub.

Also, one time I organised a sports event on one of our

weekends where we all took part in different sports and during the swimming event, I got pushed in the pool fully clothed, wallet, phone and all. The next morning, I was looking for the person who pushed me in only to find him still asleep in bed so I emptied a whole bucket of ice over him.

On another weekend after a session making cocktails Coxy said he wanted to have his ears pierced so we did it there and then with a cocktail stick. That same night we crept into my roommate's bedroom while he was asleep and stuffed all the cherries and fruit from the cocktails down the back of his underpants. In the morning I told him I was going down for breakfast. He was about to get up when he felt the back of his pants and told me that he would catch up with me later. He thought he had done something very childish.

Yet another time which I found amusing was when I roomed with Jim. I got back after him to find him sat bolt upright in bed, glasses on the end of his nose, pen in hand, halfway through filling in one of the clues in the Telegraph crossword. Only trouble was, he was fast asleep.

We also did occasional trips with the Devon Dumpling to France to play golf. Plymouth to Roscoff ferry, six hours each way, for a few days of golf. One time we stopped on the way back at a wine store. We loaded up and the driver said he didn't have the keys, he thought Tony G had them. Tony was looking for the keys in the back seat of the van when the driver found the keys and set off. Tony was still looking for the keys muttering to himself that he never had the keys. He carried on looking and muttering and by now we were miles down the road, he didn't understand why we were all laughing at him. Nowadays we all go to Portugal for a week's golf. My job while we are there is to be the bookmaker, I set the odds and everybody the night before has a bet on who they think will win. One year they told me who had won, and I checked, luckily, I had just about broken even. However, when they made the official announcement, I discovered they had wound me up. The winner was in fact a twenty-five to one outsider and two people had bet on him. I had to go down to the hole in the wall to get enough money to pay them out.

Richard, Paul and I went to France one year with a professional who wasn't particularly good. In fact on a par three all of us except the pro hit the green, to which Paul asked the pro, "Remind me again what you do for a living." We all laughed but the pro didn't.

Another pro-am the three of us entered was at Torquay. I hit my first drive badly, only about 150 yards. Paul hit his first three tee shots out of bounds so was now hitting his seventh shot off the first tee. It was now Richard's turn and his first shot hit the lady's tee and rebounded into the garden behind. Things didn't get much better and we came thirty-third out of thirty-three teams. As an apology we took the pro out and got him drunk, his wife has since banned him from playing with us again.

On another trip to France, I pinched my colleague's underwear and as we went round I took the flags off the flagpoles and replaced them with their underwear, which they found as they were in the group following me. They got me back by undoing every screw and bolt in my trolley so that when I went to pull it the whole thing collapsed.

Paul was one of the first to have an electric trolley and the first time we were in France he plugged it in and fused the whole hotel. Before trolleys, we would carry our bags, thirty-six holes a day after very late nights. God knows how.

We also tried golf in Ireland. We had a target of how many pints of Guinness we could drink in a weekend. I can't remember what the target was, but I know we reached it having our first pint at the airport at eight o'clock in the morning.

The next few years went by without any incident. I was still dating Jacky and regularly seeing the children. I didn't mention earlier but both Leanne and Daniel went to Torre

Primary School and while they were there, I spent hours making a daybook where I went in and photographed every child, teachers and events. I carefully put the book together and printed off enough copies for every child and teacher in the school to have one. Unfortunately, one of the teachers did not check the names under his class's photographs and a few had the wrong name under the wrong photograph. Disappointing after the time I had spent on this book. They both went on to Cuthbert Mayne senior school but as I wasn't impressed with Torre school Ben went to Cockington Pimary School and as a result could not get into Cuthbert Mayne and went to a private school in Teignmouth called Trinity.

Moving on to the year 2004, disaster struck and very sadly my mother died. It was such a shock as she was so healthy. When I got the phone call from the warden, I thought he had got it wrong and asked him, "Don't you mean my father?" Apparently, she got out of bed in the morning and just collapsed and died of a heart attack. What I wasn't prepared for was after the cremation, when I went to pick up her ashes, they were just handed to me in a small box. I struggled to carry this box down to where we were going to bury it, as I just kept looking at the box and thinking to myself "My mum is in here."

About three years prior to her death, she had had a large embolism and no surgeon would operate as she was too old and the embolism was too large. She eventually found one who would operate but told her she only had a 25% chance of survival, however she decided to go ahead. Prior to the operation she had written to request what she wanted in the event of her death, fortunately she survived but we still had a list of her requests which we could follow when she died. I wrote a eulogy for her funeral service but could not bring myself to read it, so the vicar did instead. She was eighty-five. RIP.

Everyone thought my father would not last long after mum died but we were proved wrong. He couldn't even boil an egg but went from strength to strength. I would phone him just about every day and if I didn't I would get an earful. He called me up one day to say he had tinnitus and he was going to see the doctor. I said I would go round later. On my arrival he said it was coming and going but kept him awake all night, with that he said it had started again "Beep, beep, beep, there it is" he said. I could also hear it and realised it was coming from the smoke detector. The batteries were dead, so I took the dead batteries out of the smoke alarm and put new ones in and told him I'd cured his tinnitus. He said, "I'll still go and see the doctor."

Another time I asked him how he was getting on with his cooking he said not very well. He told me he had put some frozen chips in the oven and when the red light came on, he took them out and he said they were all soggy and cold. I had to explain to him that the red light came on when the oven was up to temperature, not when the meal was cooked.

Shortly after mother died, I went with Dad, Julie, Dawn and their families to Tunisia on holiday. I wasn't due to go as mum was due to go but dad still wanted to go so, I went as his carer. Whilst there I took him out nearly every day and I think in the circumstances he really enjoyed himself. As it was an all-inclusive holiday, and the food was getting a little samey I arranged to take everyone out to a floating restaurant. On the way there I had booked a table outside a bar for drinks and for us to try a shisha. It was hilarious passing the pipe around and for a while dad forgot his troubles.

Dad enjoyed the trip so much he wanted another holiday the following year and it was decided on Ibiza. As my sisters enjoyed lying in the sun, I hired a car and took dad out most days and in fact he joined me to drive my buggy while I played golf. He scared me to death as he got the brake and accelerator mixed up and nearly drove it into a wall. He also drove over ladies' tee boxes and when I asked him to drive the buggy to where I hit my ball he went in the wrong direction. I did manage to get him to play one hole and he really enjoyed his day. One day we all went to a hippy market and I got dad to have his caricature drawn. When dad died the only thing I asked for from his flat was this caricature which is now proudly hanging in my office.

One night I managed to get Dawn to come out with me and we went to a karaoke bar. After a few drinks I persuaded Dawn to sing “Shout” by Lulu which she had done many times before and after a few more drinks the DJ called her up to sing her song. He gave her the microphone and she started this song very loudly “WEEEEEEEELL" and was just about to go into the “You make me want to shout” when the music started and she realised the DJ had put on a totally different version, Spanish I think. Dawn put the microphone down and came over to me. “We’re leaving”, she said.

A special Mum & Dad

Brother Roger &Sister-in - Law Ross

Sister Julie& Brother-in-Law Mike

Sister Dawn & Brother-in-Law Arthur

Jacky with her daughter Lucy & son James

Sea Moods

Spanish Home

12

USA

I had a dabble as a racehorse owner. I say racehorse owner but with the first horse I was just one of a consortium, I think I owned the horse's tail. It was called Saffa and did okay but never actually won, even though we had a leading jockey, Peter Scudemore on board. After the consortium with Saffa had finished I had a phone call from a bookmaker friend of mine, Joe who told me him and two other bookmakers were going to buy a racehorse out of France, and would I like a quarter share? The idea was they were going to bring the horse over from France, have it trained up to a high standard and then enter it for a race at a small racecourse and all of us put heavy bets on it. I agreed to come on board.

As agreed, the racehorse was quietly trained up to a high standard and entered in a race in Wales. He was at an extremely high price and had it won I stood to win over £10,000 and if he came second or third, I would win £3,000. The other bookies and even the trainer bet a lot more than I did. Unfortunately, the horse came fourth, and consequently the bookmakers had shown their hand and didn't want to pursue the horse any further. A friend of mine, Richard was interested in horseracing at that time and we decided to keep the horse with a half share each. We sent the horse to England's top trainer Martin Pipe and with England's top jockey Tony McCoy it won three races in its first season. On his last race of the season the horse, which was called Aversaksa fell, jumped over the barrier and ran into the woods. When they found him he had a nasty gash on his leg. We kept him for a while after that, but he was never the same, in fact the following year in the first two races when the tapes went up all the horses went forward and Aversaksa planted his front legs and refused to move. Hence the stewards warned us, and we had to stop racing and took him to point to point racing but that also didn't work. It was an extremely expensive hobby to keep a racehorse and even though he won three times I still only broke even on that year, so we gave him to the stable lad. I would say that nothing gets the adrenaline flowing as much as seeing your horse coming up the winning straight in the lead with thousands of people cheering. You get ten minutes of glory when you go in the winner's enclosure and receive the trophy and pose with the horse in front of loads of photographers.

As a result of being involved in racing I was asked if I would like to be an extra in an Agatha Christie film called "Ordeal by Innocence" staring Donald Sutherland. During the horse racing scene, I occasionally pop up, even once with Donald Sutherland.

I was making annual trips to the USA where a few of us would go to Myrtle Beach in South Carolina where there were 105 golf courses within a forty-five minute drive of the hotel. I started going with my brother who was still working for British Airways and got a fairly good discount on my flights. Then one year I asked a friend of mine Paul if he would like to go with me as a birthday treat. I said I would pay for the airfare, he asked me how long we would be going for and I said just a long weekend. As we were driving to the airport, I told him it was for a week and after the plane took off told him it was for ten days. He had already asked me what type of clothes he should pack, and I told him it would be really hot, so just bring shorts and t-shirts. Well South Carolina was hit with one of the worst hurricanes for years and we had to buy warm clothes and use the shorts and t-shirts as underwear.

On another trip I was swimming in the ocean when I noticed everyone was getting out of the water and the life-guard was blowing his whistle and pointing at me. I have never swum so fast and when I got to shore the lifeguard told me there was something huge coming along feeding which could have been a shark.

For a few years six of us from Torquay, plus Roger and four of his mates from Berkshire would go to South Carolina. There was a lady in the hotel in Myrtle Beach who organised all the golf for us and I thought it would be nice to treat her to something very English, so I took with me scones, strawberry jam and clotted cream. She was away that week, so I sent it to her house. The reply came back that the cookies were nice, the jelly was okay, but the butter was too sweet.

It then just became a bunch of us from Torquay who would go regularly. On one of these trips Paul and Richard were flying off to a conference for two days elsewhere in the USA. The night before they left, we had all been out for a meal and as the meals in the USA are so large, I could not finish them all and I asked for my porkchops, which were smothered in garlic, to be put in a doggy bag to take home. That night I secretly hid these porkchops in Paul's case so of course when he got to his conference all his clothes were smelling of garlic. Just another practical joke.

One year Roger didn't come and one of his mates said he would bring along his friend who turned out to be Andrew Ridgley of Wham fame. I must have done something right because the following year Andrew organised the same trip for his friends to go and specifically asked me to join them. He was not particularly easy to get on with and would shout, swear and throw his golf clubs if he made a bad golf shot.

When about to go out for a game of golf in Florida I saw a sign which said, on the ninth hole please play from the lady's tee. Being inquisitive, when I got to the ninth hole, I walked up to the men's tee to see the biggest alligator I had ever seen lying across it. Another day there was a nest of small alligators beside the fairway with the sign, these gators won't hurt you, but their mother will.

Roger was once driving with me in South Carolina when he was stopped for speeding and fined $100 but given a court date if he wanted to contest it. By that date we had come back to England, so I got a friend to phone him on the day of his court hearing and with an American accent ask him why he hadn't attended court, and say that because he hadn't he was going to be banned from entering the USA again. Roger was going along with this until my friend said he had a lot of complaints about the police officer, and he had been sacked. Roger immediately twigged they don't use the word sacked in the USA, it's fired. On a similar note, the first time I ever watched an American football match on TV the commentator said that the quarterback had been sacked five times and I thought he had a strange boss till I realised it meant he had been tackled five times.

I then decided it would be nice to own a place in Florida so after one of our tours of South Carolina I had arranged to fly down to Florida for several viewings of properties along the west coast of Florida. A friend of mine Tony said he would like to join me, together we viewed all the properties but each one had a problem, so I made no offers. Before we returned to the UK, he wanted to visit some friends of his through the music industry who lived just outside Brandon, near to Tampa. I agreed and we stayed in Treasure Island and went over to see them. There was a golf course there and me and Tony were invited to play on it by someone he knew called Jeff. Whilst playing I was talking to Jeff who happened to be an estate agent and told him that I was looking for a property, he said "Why don't you buy one here?" I replied that the ones I could see were worth between $500,000 and $1 million, out of my price range. He said he would show me a couple that weren't in that price range, so he did. After showing me them both which I liked he told me they were both under offer, disappointed we left and returned to the UK. About four or five days later I got a phone call from Jeff asking if I was still interested and when I said yes, he replied "Get your cheque book out." The deal on one of the houses I had viewed had fallen through, so I went back to Florida and bought the house.

After the deal had gone through, we went back again in order to buy the furniture. I found a very nice dining table and six chairs and it was reduced considerably because it had some scratches on it. I agreed to buy it on condition it would fit where I wanted it, we shook hands and I said I would be back in a couple of hours. On my return I saw a sold sign on it but they had sold the furniture to someone else. I called the manager and told him in the UK a handshake was a deal and unless he sorted it out I would sue (in the USA you can sue for anything). I said I was returning in six weeks and when I returned there was a knock on my door and some men delivered a brand-new identical dining table with eight chairs, which was valued at three times that of the scratched one but I was charged no extra.

I would go over every year, sometimes twice and stay at my house in River Hills. Jacky would come with me and on one occasion her family as well and on other occasions my family would come. We would get up in the morning and walk across the golf course looking out for crocodiles and birds of prey, as well as herons and their little ones. It was idyllic. There were fantastic beaches all about one hour's drive away. Clearwater, St Pete's Beach, Sarasota and our favourite, Anna Marie Island where I would sit on the pier with a cold beer fishing. We would also occasionally go down to see the Manatees, hundreds of them would come to swim in the warm water being discharged from a factory. Evenings were spent finding different restaurants, in all the years of going I never had a bad meal.

Earlier on when I had only owned the house for a couple of years, I invited my golfing buddies over to stay at the house and we had a Ryder Cup type competition against the Americans. A few weeks before this trip some people had rented the house and told the water board they were leaving, so during our visit the water board came and cut the water off whilst we were out playing golf. For the next three days we had no water and each morning walked down to the golf clubhouse for showers etc. On another occasion my brother and his wife came over and we went to a Japanese restaurant where we had to share a table with two girls. They were taking part in a karaoke competition and asked us to go along and support them, which we did. When we got to the pub they had a very nice cider on draught which we took advantage of. When we left, although probably over the limit I felt fine, I thought it was only a mile up the road so I stupidly drove. After about a quarter of a mile the police were pulling everyone into a car park to breathalyse them, so I thought the worst. For some unknown reason when they got to me, they waved me on and then stopped every car behind me so I was driving up a totally empty road. I was still shaking when I got back to the house. Never again.

At one time over there with Daniel we had to drive to Clearwater to pick up some furniture. We were told we would have to wait an hour while they sorted it out and the only place we could go to was McDonald's, yuck! Whilst in there a very large lady came by carrying two trays of the biggest burgers I've ever seen and two huge piles of chips on each one, together with two bucketsful of Coca-Cola. We both turned around to see if the lady she'd bought the other items for was as big as her, only to find this lady was on her own and she ate the lot, unbelievable.

I did some work on the house by extending the lanai at the back by about twenty feet. This virtually made another room, so we always went outside for breakfast and sometimes had a barbecue out there. While the barbecue was heating up Jacky and I would play the sixteen hole which was directly behind the house. The wildlife was fantastic, when the eagles had little ones if you went anywhere near their nest, they would just circle overhead keeping an eye on you. Once a huge black snake came close, although I understand it was harmless, but the best was finding an alligator on my front lawn.

I have over the years made many friends over there and the local pub called the Landings was a particularly favourite place and we would regularly call in on our way home. For supper one night me and James ordered a few chicken wings and nachos. When they arrived, they filled two enormous trays, enough for eight people. I intend calling my new house in Spain “The Landings” in order to remind me of the fun times I had in Florida.

At the local golf club at River Hills I was once asked to do some magic for the male members that had had a lot to drink, I was quite nervous but it went down very well. It must have because six weeks later when I was in a pub in Brandon a man came up to me and said, "I remember you you're the magic man." (small world). Another time we were invited to a party and I was again asked to do some magic, after which the host offered to fly me back later in the year to do a magic show for his daughter’s birthday. I didn’t take up his offer.

13
ANOTHER PROJECT

I carried on working to improve and extend Oldway Heights. It was originally two buildings joined together with a single-storey connection, so I drew up plans to put a second storey on top of the connection and put a second lift in. I eventually got this passed by the planners and had it built. Unfortunately, I chose the wrong builder and have had many structural problems ever since. Next, I built the sun lounge and then wanted to put on three more bedrooms. The back garden area took for ever to get permission and in the end had to put in a soak-away the size of half of the garden. However due to perseverance and a lot of sleepless nights I now have forty-one bedrooms in the home, forty of which are en-suite, and in the garden on the patio I now have a hot tub and a gazebo, both of which are very popular with the residents.

I had a young resident who had been involved in a motorbike accident and was now a tetraplegic. He was on no medication except he would smoke up to five cannabis cigarettes a day which alleviated his pain. Being worried about this I phoned the police who told me that what happened behind his closed door was nothing to do with me as long as no staff helped him in any way. A few weeks later on my birthday I was conducting a residents meeting and I thought it was funny, there were a lot of staff present. However, I carried on until a policewoman arrived and came over and whispered in my ear that she was part of the drug squad. I was petrified until the music started and she was a stripogram organised by my staff and residents for my birthday. Sadly, the resident mentioned died quite young. I was just going into the funeral service when his family asked me to say a few words at the service, so I hurriedly conjured up an eulogy. I mentioned in my eulogy how he was a very quiet person and wouldn't even tell me what the sweet smell of tobacco coming from its room was, which caused a few smiles from his relatives. On the same subject, over the years I have had two residents die whose relatives refused to pay for a vicar so I got up behind the pulpit at the crematorium and took the service myself. The funeral directors on both occasions congratulated me.

So now my next project starts, I am told that I'm never happy unless I've got a project on the go. I was looking to move back to Torquay and as my finances were picking up, I started to look for a move. Around this time the well-known Brent group of hotels had a subsidiary company which wanted to buy Oldway Mansion and approached me with the view of buying Little Oldway as well. They were very keen and offered me £1.3 million which I accepted. However when I saw the contract they said they were going to have some retirement flats built near the road, build houses on the way up to Oldway Mansion, then renovate the mansion to a five star hotel and finally convert Little Oldway. This was going to take five years and I had no objection to the building they anticipated, however the contract stated that during that time they wanted me to run Little Oldway as a care home for them, which I refused. It was a blessing in disguise because the following year they pulled out of the whole deal. The problem was that I had committed myself to move to Torquay and was going to use some of the balance of the money to buy a house. The money from the sale of Monterey House had been used to buy a house for Jackie P so I was going to have to obtain a giant mortgage.

Regarding the move, I couldn't find anything I liked and when I upped my budget, I was being sent six or seven bedroom houses or sent out to Marine Drive/Thatcher area which is quite a long way out. I then came across Sea Moods which was vastly overpriced, but the views were spectacular, and my mind was racing how I could convert it to exactly what I wanted. The house used to be owned by the neighbour who had his present house built in the grounds. He would explain a few things to me which later I found to be untrue, but I still bought it and embarked on the plans.

All the way through the planning stage I had trouble with the neighbour and things only got worse during the build. I wanted a curved front on the house and the architect thought it would not work, they said I should angle it like a 50p coin but I insisted on the curved one. There were many consultations with the architect as I had a different design in mind, but in the end I got what I wanted. From day one of the build, I had problems with the neighbour and at one stage he halted proceedings. He didn't like the balcony and took me to court. I gave in a little too soon on this one as I wanted to get on with the build and it was agreed to put up a screen. However, this did not stop him, and he complained about everything, mainly saying that I had breached some of the covenants. This time I was not going to back down and we finished up in high court. He claimed the site was untidy, parking in the wrong place, building in front of the building line (which was some underground bricks under a manhole cover) and six other breaches of covenant. The judge came down from Exeter to see the problems and opened his address in court by saying he could not see any problems. At one stage he asked my neighbour about my drive and my neighbour replied that it was unsightly. The judge had taken a photo that morning and showed it to my neighbour asking where the drive was and course it was totally hidden.

After four days in court with both of us having solicitors and barristers it was clear he was losing the case and made me an offer which I did not accept, he then upped his offer many times and then I realised that if we did not settle the next court hearing would not be for three months. I finally settled, he had to pay all his own costs, nearly all my costs, and the court costs totalling £115,000. I had already paid my solicitor over the preceding year and got all that back except for about £8,000 which I would have got if I had agreed to come back to court in three months time, but the stress was enormous, so I settled. Shortly after the court case my neighbour moved but not before he upset the new owner of his house.

It was now time to furnish the house which I mainly sourced locally except for a few items bought on the internet and the dining table bought from Harrods. What I tended to do was, if I saw something I liked I decided where it should go, rather than just go out looking for an item of furniture. So slowly I furnished the home. Another item I bought from Harrods was an enormous mirror clock which showed the time in three different countries. I like the idea of knowing what the time is in America and in Thailand. The clock was so heavy my handyman from work and my son put it up, unfortunately the minute hand on the main clock kept getting caught on the minute hand of one of the smaller clocks. I complained to Harrods and they told me to have it checked locally, which I refused because it might invalidate the guarantee. They then said they would get some new hands from Italy, which they did. Then they phoned me and said they were going to send the whole clock back to Italy. This had gone on for several months so before it went back to Italy, I decided to read the installation instructions which clearly said, when you first put the clock up you should line the minute and the hour hand together showing twelve o'clock. This hadn't been done, so I did this and the clock worked perfectly. I told Harrods the new hands solved the problem, even though I hadn't even taken them out of the box.

Another incident which involved Harrods was when I was watching a demonstration in the store of how to use a magic box and I was quite impressed. At Christmas there it was, a present from Jacky. Unfortunately, one of the tricks broke so I phoned Harrods, who were full of apologies and sent me a totally new magic box. It wasn't until some months later at a dinner party that Jacky told me and everyone else there that she had not bought it from Harrods but from the QVC shopping channel.

I had always been interested in magic, so I then started buying CDs, books and watching tricks on the internet. I got reasonably confident, mainly with playing cards. I was invited to a Magic Circle meeting as an observer, there were about twenty magicians there. We sat on tables of four and each in turn did a trick in front of everyone on the table and then everyone moved to another table and did the same trick again to different magicians. This went on until everyone had seen everyone else's tricks and a vote was taken whose was the best trick. Someone who wanted to join the Magic Circle had to do a ten minute show in front of all the magicians and on the strength of that show they voted whether he would be accepted. After the meeting I was asked if I wanted to join but I declined as I felt I wasn't good enough to perform in front of semi-professional and professional magicians.

One example of me not being good enough was when a friend's son was getting married and he asked me if I could do a show at the wedding breakfast, after they finished the food but before the group played. My first trick involved someone coming onto the stage, picking a card, showing everyone except me the card, then putting it back in the pack. I would then throw the whole pack at the window and the card the person picked would be stuck to the outside of the glass. All hundred people were watching, and when the wrong card stuck to the window everybody laughed. At this point the audience seem to lose interest and it took me a long time to win them back. After this I just kept to entertaining guests after we put on dinner parties.

After seeing Jacky for many years, she moved in with me which made life a lot easier and more stable. This had been on the cards for some time as we were both running separate homes and it would be nice to come home from work to company. Not like a few weeks previous when I was sat in on my own and thought I would go down to the pub for a bit of company and finished up talking with someone about his love for tractors. I went home and told myself that it was time to sort myself out. So, Jacky and I had a long chat and as a result she moved in.

They were asking me to dance with them

She said put the tip where you like

Me & Jacky

Riding a Snowman

Do anything to get in the frame

Black Lives Matter

The one that didn't get away

I didn't tell her the elephant was about to charge

Pantomime time

Dying in the desert

14
BIRTHDAYS

As my finances were getting more secure, we started travelling. I decided it might be an idea to buy an apartment in Spain which would be a lot easier to get to than Florida. It was also my intention to occasionally take residents from Oldway Heights over there on holiday, so eventually bought a two bed, two bathroom apartment in Puerto de la Duquesa. Over the years we went over many times, we also took family and friends and on four occasions took residents from Oldway Heights. By going over so frequently I got to know all the places in the area well.

I have always tried to celebrate my milestone birthdays in a good fashion. For my fortieth I booked Churston Court Hotel for about eighty people, taking sixty of them in a coach from Torquay. Having a lot of friends who are musicians, music was no problem. The only problem was that when I came back from holiday three days before, to my dismay I read in the evening paper the Churston Court Hotel had lost its licence. I overcame this by having a free bar and of course no closing time so went on till about four o'clock in the morning. The coach driver was not amused.

My fiftieth was held at Monterey House. I had the chefs

from work put on the buffet and had a singer who have just won a TV talent show. My parents asked to come but little did I know the lads from the pub had organised a stripogram and while she was performing who should be sitting in the front row but my mother and father.

For my sixtieth I had booked Dartmouth golf club and hotel for sixty guests for two nights. On the second day we had a golf tournament and at night we had a party and again I had a singer and put together a band. After playing in the band, they hit me with brandies, tequilas and everything else. I was in a dreadful state and this was the first time I met Joe my future son-in-law, so I don't know what he thought of me, they all tied some gas balloons to me to try and keep me upright.

My seventieth birthday was twofold, firstly ten of us went over to Marbella for five days, having a different event each day finishing with a party at Nikki Beach. On the morning of the party my knee was so painful I could not get out of bed. A doctor was called who gave me an injection and within an hour I joined all my friends who were surprised to see me. Even though it rained we had a great time, finishing up in the swimming pool.

I had been to Nikki Beach before when I was invited by a friend of mine, John M, to his son's thirtieth birthday party. Jacky and I happened to be in Spain at that time so we reluctantly agreed to go as it was family only and we were the only non-family there. John asked me if I would bring a few cards to do some tricks. On arrival John asked me to sit next to his brother-in-law Tom and sister Marilyn. I was doing a particular trick with Marilyn where she could tell the truth or tell me a lie. Each time she told me a lie I called her a liar, and everyone around was laughing. I did this a few times and after I'd finished the trick found out that the Tom I was sitting next to was Sir Tom Hunter. His wife was Lady Hunter, and it was Lady Hunter that I was calling a liar. Sir Tom in fact at one time was one of the wealthiest men in Scotland, worth over a billion pounds. The first time I met John M was many years before on Christmas Eve when he was introduced to me and bought everyone except me a drink. He was so embarrassed later because the others had told him I was teetotal. I often remind him of this.

The second part of my seventieth birthday celebration involved me taking all my family to Tenerife. On my actual birthday when I went down to breakfast, they were all wearing face masks with my face on it. They also organised a surprise dinner which was a tremendous evening. I just love being with my family.

Due to my love of music, I have been to Glastonbury Festival on three occasions. The first time I went with Jacky when Stevie Wonder was headlining. We went in a seven berth Winnebago and had to park it some way away from the main site. Ben, Daniel, Leanne and their partners were all camping down on the main site. In the morning they would come up to see us and Jacky gave them a cooked breakfast and they used our shower. The problem was by the time everyone had had a shower there was no hot water left when it was mine and Jacky's turn.

The second time I went with a friend of mine, John W, this time in a smaller campervan but again we had to park it away from the site. After each day, bearing in mind we had quite a few beers, we had trouble finding the campervan and seem to go round and round in circles. On our way back it was quite muddy underfoot. John had Wellington boots and I said, "These old golf shoes with spikes on are much better". As soon as I said that I fell flat on my face in the mud.

When watching "Chic", a rather plump lady asked John if she could get on his shoulders to see better. He agreed but I could see his eyes popping out of his head as he lifted her, then she started dancing and he couldn't keep his feet it was so funny to watch.

The third time I went with John and also Alan and his wife

Gina. While the Rolling Stones were on and about 120,000 people watching them you couldn't get in or out so if you wanted a wee you just used an empty plastic pint pot and then discreetly tipped it onto the grass. While I was using one Daniel turned around to me as he felt something trickling down the back of his leg. My plastic pot had a crack in it.

One afternoon whilst walking around Glastonbury I heard a ten-piece swing band. I bought myself a pint of cider and sat on a bale of hay for an hour listening to them. Three or four pints of cider later I closed my eyes and imagined them playing on my front lawn. When they finished, I went and got their details. The following year I put up a huge marquee on my front lawn and booked this same swing band to come and play. I invited all my friends and neighbours, certainly an afternoon to remember.

My brother Roger had been with his lady Ross for many years and had been through the blessing in front of the monks in Thailand. This however was not recognised under English law, so he decided to come over to the UK to get married, the date was set for the 31st of May, his seventieth birthday. I arranged with the registrar for that date and also arranged where we were going to have the wedding breakfast and the evening do, as well as sorting the invitations. When Roger came over to the UK, he found out he had to be in the country for fourteen days before he could get married. The fourteenth day was the 1st of June so the evening do became his birthday party and I had to rearrange the wedding breakfast, although the serviettes etc at the wedding breakfast all had the wrong date on. I tried to help Ross with the pronunciation of her vows but no matter how I tried she was unable to say the word solemnly. My part in the wedding was driving Roger to the registry office, giving Ross away, being best man and organising the photographs. I am not sure if I finished up marrying her myself. However a great day and a great couple.

In my life I have been best man at weddings seven times,

three of them for Roger. Me and three of my friends, Richard, Mike and Paul all club together to do something for each other's special birthdays. For mine they took me to Bournemouth for a weekend of golf. Paul organised his own trip and a whole bunch of us went to Mojacar for a week. For Mike we went on a day's sailing in a tall ship sailing yacht. We all went to Oxford for Richard's treat, to the headquarters of Webber barbecues where they showed us how to correctly cook on a barbecue and from twelve noon till four o'clock drinks were free. A young boy's job was washing up and serving drinks, during this time needless to say not much washing up got done. In the evening we went to a pub in Oxford which was full of students and got talking to them. When they asked why we were in Oxford I told them I was the cox in the 1970 boat race. On hearing this they were quite excited until one asked me which university I was in and when I told them they all laughed, and my cover was blown because that was a girls-only university.

One day at Oldway Heights the clothes dryer in the laundry room caught fire. At this time I had a small lounge at the end of the building to which all the residents were taken, and the Fire Brigade were called. It was during the fireman's strike so they sent a Green Goddess which was so old it couldn't get up Headland Park Road and had to go around the houses, anyway they sorted it and there wasn't too much damage.

On another day at Oldway Heights there was an ex-alcoholic who had been told if he drank again it would kill him. He seemed to ignore this warning and one morning he went out and could hardly stand on his return. My care manager put him to bed and told the carers to check him every fifteen minutes. While the carers were helping with the lunch my care manager went up to see him and came down to say his heart and breathing had stopped and he had died. While she was phoning the doctor I went into his room and administered

CPR on him, after about five minutes his head moved, he took one breath and stopped again. I slapped his face and carried on with CPR. After what seemed like ages he came round, and I lay him on the floor in the recovery position. When the paramedics arrived, they congratulated me. A real job satisfaction day.

I had a resident who was in his late 80s and during his life had been a very good sportsman representing Devon in three different sports and at golf still playing off a single figure handicap while in his 70s. I would chat with him most days about politics and sport, then put a chair a short way down the corridor and he would try and walk to it. One day he collapsed and when we brought him round he just swore at us as he had had enough of life. A few days later he got his wish and died. This in fact gave me hope that when my body wears out I will be ready to meet my maker, but hopefully not for many years.

All four of us along with our partners went to the Savoy hotel London for an all-afternoon lunch. We had what was called The Chef's Table, around which there were just eight of us in a room overlooking the kitchens. For each separate course a different chef would come in and explain to us how it was cooked. Each course was accompanied by a bottle of wine, and there were seven courses. For the main course we were invited into the kitchen to cook our own steaks which was quite a thrill. You had to do a countdown "four minutes chef, three minutes chef, two minutes chef" and then when it was ready you took it out to the serving counter and shouted "Service". Me and Jacky stayed at the Savoy overnight as I had accumulated a shed load of nectar points which paid for it. Jacky was looking in the hotel jewellery department when the assistant showed her a diamond necklace which was for sale for £50,000 and asked "Would madam like to borrow it for the evening?" She declined the invitation.

After mum died as I said dad continued in good health and took part in just about every social activity that was held in the lounge of the warden-controlled flats where he lived. For his ninety-fifth birthday we put on a party in the communal lounge. All the residents of the other flats attended and when he walked into the lounge, he was so popular that they all stood up to clap and cheer him. Sadly, he died on Valentine's Day 2010 at the age of ninety-seven, up until a month or so before he died, he still had a good quality of life. I remember on visiting him in hospital that morning I received a phone call from Joe asking me if I would give my blessing for him to marry Leanne, so I had a mixture of emotions that day. I wrote a eulogy for his funeral service which my brother read out. It started with, "I never knew my father till he was sixty-five" which was true mainly because he was always working but on his sixty-fifth birthday I organised a surprise party for his retirement and after that we became best of buddies. Dad at parties after a few drinks would always give us a rendition of two songs, one of which was Eleven More Months and Ten More Days. So after he died we had a wake, and I distributed the song sheets to everyone so we could all sing this song in his memory.

15

WEDDINGS & TRAVELLING

Every year I make a trip to Thailand to see my brother who after all is my best friend. I get a lot of raised eyebrows when I go, and Jacky hates me going. It is all to do with the reputation and stigma that goes on in Thailand but I just say unless you want your bits to fall off you stay clear of all the temptations. Whilst out there I did join a company consortium to buy some building land, however another developer was worried we were going to build an estate near to his, so he bought the land from us and I subsequently doubled my investment. Along with my brother we then bought a smaller piece of land between us on which to build five houses. I subsidised the building costs and when it was finished and all the houses sold, I had my investment repaid and we split the profit.

In order to get the money back to the UK I offered expats a better exchange rate than the banks. After they put the sterling into my account my brother paid them in bhats out of my profit.

Roger lived about eight kilometres out of town and on my first visit to his new house he dropped me off in town and said he would be back at 2 pm and meet him outside Mike's store. At 2 pm no sign of Roger, nor at 3 pm or 4pm. So there I was, not knowing where Roger lived, no money in my pocket and no phone. By five o'clock panic was setting in so I sat down to try and calm myself and have a bite to eat. During my meal I saw Roger drive past, so I leapt up and chased after him. Luckily, there was a traffic jam, so I caught up with him. It transpired that there was a small Mike's store at one end of the town and a large department store called Mike's at the other end where I was waiting while Roger was at the small one. It was a good job there was a traffic jam or I would still be there now.

A couple of years later I recall one night while Roger still lived out of town we were out together with some friends when Roger went home early, and I said I would catch up later. About 1am I flagged down a motorbike taxi and told him to take me out to the main road, turn left and after about eight kilometres I would direct him. How I did it I don't know but I fell asleep on the back of the motorbike. When the driver woke me up after eight kilometres I had no idea where I was, so I had to phone my brother. Apparently, the motorbike driver had turned right instead of left at the main road, so I was now sixteen kilometres away on this little moped. However, Roger guided us in and I got back at about 4 am.

On another occasion we went over to one of the islands and at one end of the beach was a whole troop of monkeys. I bought some bananas and was feeding them when a little baby monkey came and sat on my lap. He sat there for ages and would not move, in the end I had to stand up and push him off whereupon he let out a squeal. The next day I went down to the same end of the beach and the monkey's mother came out of nowhere and hit me in the back as hard as she could.

On my return from Thailand one year, I was driving back home from Heathrow Airport listening to a programme on Radio Five Live about care homes. I was so incensed by the way the debate was going I phoned them. They said if they wanted to use me, they would phone back. I was just at the garage getting petrol when the phone rang, "This is Radio Five Live. Please turn off any radios you are about to go live on the radio." Bearing in mind I had been up for the last twenty-four hours it probably wasn't the best of ideas, but I think I coped. This happened again sometime later with another radio channel but on a different subject, still to do with the care home industry. As a result of my input to that debate I was asked to go on TV to discuss this issue, but I declined.

Another time I was asked to go on TV was for a program called “Come dine with me” they phoned me out of the blue, asked me questions and as a result phoned back twice and then the producer phoned me. I told them the kitchen in my new house wasn't ready and she even asked if I could use someone else's house and kitchen but again I refused.

It was exciting times over the next few years as my three children got married. Leanne's wedding was at Powderham Castle and together we drove in an old-fashioned car and got there a little early, so we sat in the back with a glass of champagne just talking. I am known for being very emotional, so I was struggling. In fact, when I made my speech after the wedding, I made a joke of it by putting on bigger and bigger sunglasses as the speech progressed to hide my emotional tears. The only problem was in front of me I had some bullet points for my speech and when I put the sunglasses on I couldn't read them.

Leanne had arranged for a tractor with a long trailer to take the guests from the church to the castle, which was about half a mile, he could take about twenty at a time. Now Powderham Castle is renowned for having many herds of deer in its grounds so I asked the tractor driver if I kept all the children till last could he drive around the grounds so they could see the deer. He did this but when he got to the furthest point from the castle the heavens opened and of course there was no roof on the trailer. All the mums who had had their hair done for the wedding got their hair ruined. I went from being the hero to being the villain.

Next was Daniel who wanted an event type wedding, so a huge marquee was erected and some of his friends camped around but most of us stayed in the farm cottages. I devised a table plan which was based on Glastonbury with models of the various stages outside each stage with little figures holding a flag with a name on it. Whichever flag your name was on you made a note of the stage you were outside. When you went in for the wedding breakfast all the tables were named after stages and you just found the table with the name of your stage on.

Finally, it was Ben's wedding held in Sorrento so we all went to Italy for a week. At the reception Nicky's father (Ben's new father-in-law) did not want to make a speech so I volunteered and made two life-size heads with moving mouths, one of Ben and one of Nicky. I played a recording of a lady with a north country Teesside accent and a man with a west country accent. This caused much hilarity but sadly the guests lost them on their drunken night out afterwards. The party continued the next day in a reserved room beside the beach. What a fabulous week.

I have over the years been involved in many carnivals, firstly as chairman of the Junior Chamber of Commerce I was asked on three consecutive years to judge the Shaldon boat carnival where the people of Shaldon would decorate their boats. One year a boat was made up to look like a biplane and it looked so authentic I thought it was a full sized biplane landing on the river. We would be taken out on the river to judge them, for the first two years after the judging we would get pelted with flower bags but as this got rather dangerous on the final year we had to judge them from the shore.

I entered floats in the Paignton carnival. My remit was we have loud music, and it was topical and fun. The first one was based on Isaac Singer's household in 1860, then we did Annus

Horribilis which was based on the dreadful year the Queen had. Windsor Castle was in the background with smoke coming out, the Queen Mother with fishbones stuck in her throat and Fergie sucking her boyfriend's toe. Then we did "I'm a Carer Get Me Out of Here", based on the TV programme. Then "The Rolling Stones Final Final Grab a granny Tour", five of us dressed up as the Rolling Stones, mimed to their music and had an audience of residents and staff throwing enormous knickers and corsets at us. Down the side we had a sign "Touring Asia, Europe, Africa and America in fact the InContinence tour. Then it was "Sister Act" we all dressed up as nuns, but I had my habit split up the back showing me wearing stockings and suspenders. Following that it was the turn of "Carers in Your Eyes", based on TV's "Stars in Your Eyes." We all took it in turns being a celebrity and miming to the music, I was Freddie Mercury. Next it was supposed to be a float based on Michael Jackson. Unfortunately the week before the procession Michael Jackson died so we changed it to a tribute to Michael Jackson, Ben was his monkey. Next was Grease and on this one and most of the others one of my staff called Debbie choreographed all the staff and residents into a great dance routine behind the float. The last entry we did was when it was pouring with rain and we were ready to go as Mary Poppins so I asked everyone, as we had won the best float trophy for the past three years, would they like to go down at 6 pm for the judging and get very wet or just join the back of the procession at 7:30. They all voted for the latter, when we had finished the procession an official from health and safety told us if he had seen us at the start he wouldn't have allowed us to take part. He wanted a barrier all around the bed of the lorry and anyone on it tied down with a chain and belt. Shame, as this was impossible, it ruined the carnival for everyone, and we never took part again.

A whole bunch of us went to Powderham Castle for a picnic in the park and in the evening, Elton John came on. We had been there most of the day and had quite a few glasses of wine with our picnic. After the concert was finished our minibus and driver came to pick us up but took nearly three hours just to get out of the venue so during that time between us, we consumed all the rest of the alcohol. On the way home I got a phone call from work asking me to go in, I said I could hardly stand so there was no chance of me coming in. Fifteen minutes later phone went again, it's urgent come into work, to which they got the same reply. Another fifteen minutes went by, phone again, so I agreed I would get the driver to drop me off at work. When I arrived, there were police everywhere and I staggered up to the front door and said to the police sergeant, "Good evening offither I am the pupproprietor but I'm sorry I have had a glass or thoo of wine." He replied that he thought I'd had more than a glass or two. Sadly, what had happened was a resident who only came to me for two weeks respite had committed suicide.

One of my favourite things to do is to go travelling. Someone once said to me on long haul if you don't fly business class your kids will so ever since I have spent some of their inheritance flying business class. Here are most of the countries I have visited: Australia, Bali, Thailand, Malaysia, India, Vietnam, Cambodia, Borneo, China, France, Spain, Portugal, Germany, USA, Nepal, Canada, Italy, Holland, Croatia, Honduras, Guatemala, Belize, Scotland, Wales, Kenya, Zambia, Zimbabwe, Bahamas, Barbados, Dominican Republic, Gibraltar, Jersey, Cuba, Belgium, Japan, Switzerland, Vatican City, Monaco, Mexico, Sicily, Philippines, Ireland, Cyprus, Singapore, UAE, Egypt, Morocco, Algeria, Tunisia, Turkey, Montenegro, Andorra, Malta, England, South Africa, Mozambique, and Namibia.

Some of these places resulted in interesting stories. On PP Island we were invited to go snorkelling which I did, but stood on a very sharp sea urchin. When getting back into the boat the captain said the only way to take the pain away was to pee on my foot, which I had to do while twenty people were on the boat. In Myrtle Beach, South Carolina I was out swimming in the sea when I heard the shrill of a whistle. I noticed everyone had got out of the sea and the life guard was pointing at me. I have never swum so fast in my life to get to the shore. The life guard told me there was a very large fish feeding near the shore which could have been a shark. In Las Vegas we stayed at the Bellagio hotel and the first night did very well playing blackjack in the casino. However the following night I went to the same table and was doing very well until a Japanese man came to the table smoking heavily, so I moved to another table and lost. The first time I went to Las Vagas which was in 1976, while I was at the tables they offered free drinks and food to me and all my guests. They would do anything to keep you in their casino. On one occasion a waitress came to ask what we all wanted to drink. Just at that point the music started, and the waitress got up onto the stage and did a strip-tease, put her clothes back on, came back to my table and just asked what was that order again? Las Vegas is a quite different place now. We then flew to San Francisco which was a fun city and whilst there included a trip to Alcatraz. The plan was then to drive down the pacific highway to Los Angeles. We drove down the beautiful coastline for thirty miles only to find the road closed due to a landslide and had to drive back. Driving over the Golden Gate Bridge you are charged a hefty toll but only one way. Because we were driving the other way I thought, great I haven't got to pay the toll. Unfortunately, when we got over, we got lost and finished up driving back over the bridge and had to pay the toll.

We were taken from San Diego on a five day trip to Baja California Sur which is a bay in Mexico. To get there it was a two and a half hour coach ride, then a two hour flight in a small plane, followed by a further half hour coach ride. We stayed in a hut which wasn't much bigger than a beach hut, the toilets were 100 yards away and you had to put your name down for a shower. The food mainly consisted of re-fried beans. This trip was very expensive, and the facilities were dreadful however I would go back in a heartbeat. The reason was for two hours every morning and two hours every afternoon we were taken out on a small boat along with six or seven other people to see the grey whales. Apparently in the bay at that time there were over 150 whales, they would come up to the boat and you could pat these thirty ton whales on the back, while their ten ton babies would swim under as though they were playing with the boat. You could watch them breaching and spy hopping right next to you, an amazing experience.

From there we flew to New Orleans for the Mardi Gras which was very exciting but so busy we could not get in the pubs and clubs to listen to the music.

When we were in Vatican City the Pope was doing his normal Sunday morning speech which we went to. Before we went, I asked the hotel if he was making his speech and they gave me a phone number to check. I always kept that number on my phone in my contacts under the heading "The Pope".

I have tried my hand at skiing on several occasions which I thoroughly enjoyed. The first time was when I went with Daniel and Ben to Andorra they took to skiing like a duck to water but I wasn't in the same league. After a few days I said to them, you go off skiing on your own but we will meet up every two hours at a certain venue. We did this for the whole day, but they did not turn up for the final meeting at our agreed rendezvous. I waited and waited and as it was beginning to get dark, I was beginning to panic. I asked a travel rep and a ski instructor, but they weren't any help whatsoever, so I came down on the last lift and the lift man was very helpful. He went and got a map of the area and showed me an area where one of the ski lifts closed early and if they were in that area at the time, they would not be able to get back to our meeting. This gave me some relief, but I was still greatly concerned. Just as I was arriving back at the hotel I saw them walking up the street, what a relief, it transpired that it had happened exactly as the lift man predicted.

Onto other occasions, we went to Courchevel twice. Jacky and I were joined on each occasion by many friends. On the second occasion we were there on New Year's Eve and in the evening after the gala dinner we had a bunfight in the restaurant against Richard Branson and his family. One of our party, Mike D was an experienced skier and would be our Red Leader when we went out. He only took us on the blue and green slopes but one day said we would have to go down a short black run during our daily trip. When we got there, he told us we would slowly zigzag down but when he took me across, I inadvertently turned my skis downwards and went down the black slope at what seem to be 100 miles an hour.

The next day I had hurt my calf muscle so had a day off from skiing. I looked out the window of the hotel to see this little plane taking off down the side of the mountain. I don't know why, but I asked reception if they did pleasure trips on that plane she came back and said yes but there had to be three of us. Jacky said she would go and at dinner that night I asked for another volunteer and Andrew agreed to come. How scary that trip was, we took off down the side of the mountain and there was a little lip at the end like on an aircraft carrier and into the air we flew, he took us up to Mont Blanc. When we came back, we landed on the same airstrip, this time going upwards and it was only gravity that stopped us.

In the evening just as it was getting dark, we would all arrange to meet in a bar partway up the mountain. After a few drinks we would all link together like a crocodile and come down the slope at some speed. I would be in the middle and just hung on for dear life.

When we went to Shizuoka in Japan, I said to Jacky the first thing I want to see is Mount Fuji, so I wanted to make inquiries of the best way of getting there, should we go by rail, bus or taxi. Jacky said, "Why don't you look over your shoulder?" I turned around only to see a perfect view of Mount Fuji. Still in Japan, we went to Osaka and had a ride on a high-speed bullet train, while it did not reach its full potential it was still very exhilarating.

In Hanoi we joined the queue to see Ho Chi Min lying in state. He died in 1969 but there is still a queue every day to see him. I thought it strange that Ho Chi Minh was lying in state in Hanoi and not in Ho Chi Minh city.

Whilst in Kenya not only did we see the endangered species of black rhinoceros but also the migrating wildebeest over the Mara river. We were very lucky as other people on safari had not seen any crossings in two weeks, we saw three crossings in one week, although you have to have a strong stomach to see the gators picking them off.

After we left Kenya we went over to Mozambique for a few days on the beach. There were only about six people staying in the hotel as the Americans had been advised not to travel to Mazambique. One day I went down to the beach and there was no one there except a local. I asked him if he knew anywhere I could go out fishing and he said he would arrange it for the next day. When I told Jacky, she was extremely concerned because right next to Mozambique is Somalia where a lot of people out on boats got kidnapped. The next day a motorboat arrived with three locals on to take me fishing. By then I was a little nervous so I asked the fishermen how far out we were going, and they confirmed we would be going just the other side of the reef. When we got over two miles past the reef my anxiety was setting in, especially when we started heading towards some run-down sailing boats. However, all ended well I caught a few fish and I got safely back. Jacky told me when I got back that she had photographed all the fishermen in case they tried to kidnap me.

. . .

In Barbados, a local gave me a joint. I took one puff, coughed my heart out and gave it to someone else.

One of the most surreal places we went was Halong Bay in Vietnam, where for two days we just drifted around these enormous rock formations coming out of the tranquil sea. In Cairns Australia I wanted to go diving over the barrier reef but as I explained earlier had a phobia about going out of my depth. On the way out to the reef we stopped to do some snorkelling, there were about twenty people snorkelling, one of whom had a lifejacket on. When I got round to diving over the reef, I had a very good instructor who guided me through and eased my concerns. In fact, when we got to the next reef, I was first in the queue to go diving again.

Singapore gets the vote for the most striking hotel we have stayed in. It was called the Marina Bay Sands and had three enormous columns which were joined together at the top a few hundred feet up by a swimming pool.

In Alaska we caught a seaplane out to a place called Lake Brooks. This was to watch the brown bears in the river catching salmon, I could have stayed there all day just watching them. We were told there was a chance a brown bear or a grizzly bear could walk past us and if one did, we should just step to one side and quietly speak to it, luckily one did not pass us.

One other place that needs a mention was in South Africa I went cage diving in with the sharks. While underwater in the cage many copper sharks came up to me, but the highlight was when a great white shark came by and even the crew on the boat cheered because they had not seen one in ages.

In Chitwan, which is a town in Nepal we came across two rhinoceroses which were just outside someone's back garden. They looked as though they were going to charge us, so we ran and hid, luckily rhinoceroses have bad eyesight. In that same town I got on the back of an elephant who took me into a river. He had been taught to suck water up his trunk and throw it over me, to the amusement of many people who were stood on the shore he then rolled to one side throwing me into the river. Not the most hygienic or safe thing I have ever done as floating down the river was great mounds of elephant dung and on the bank on the other side were probably ten or twenty alligators.

I would add that I had done a total of three scenic railway journeys. Before I met Jacky. I went on the Orient Express from London to Paris, they were so free-flowing with the champagne I was tipsy before we left London.

Jacky and I went on the Rocky Mountaineer in Canada which was absolutely brilliant. We sat upstairs, the carriage was nearly all glass, the views were outstanding, mountain rivers etc. This was a two-day trip, staying in a hotel overnight.

The third journey was on The Blue Train from Cape Town to Johannesburg which again was a two-day trip, this time sleeping on the train. The food and service (with the exception of our butler) was first class, but we were disappointed with the views and the whole trip didn't live up to the Rocky Mountaineer standards.

Fate seems to follow me round on some of my trips. Two weeks after leaving Bali the terrorists blew up the nightclub we passed most days. In Barcelona, the Catalonians came out on the street demonstrating and it was close to being a riot. We stayed at the Taj Mahal Palace in Delhi which had been attacked by terrorists a few years earlier and there were still bullet holes in some areas. Whilst in Hamburg, Germany for New Year, refugees and asylum seekers went on the rampage with reports of looting theft and rape, fortunately we didn't know anything about this until the next day. A week after we were in Kathmandu they were hit by a terrible earthquake and we saw pictures of places we had been to which were now razed to the ground. Coming into land on a plane once we were just about to touchdown when the pilot saw something on the runway, had to abort the landing, and seemed to take to the air vertically. In Dubai because we had stayed in the same hotel twice, we looked at a hotel across the road called The Address, with a view of staying there next time we were in Dubai. The following New Year's Eve I was watching TV at home and they were showing a hotel in Dubai on fire and sure enough it was the hotel we were going to stay in. There was of course the incident on the Zambezi River which I mentioned earlier.

I am often asked of all the places I have been to which is my favourite? This is very difficult to answer as if you want stunning scenery then Alaska is hard to beat with the rivers, mountains and glaciers. If it's a great climate and beautiful beaches, then it's Barbados. If it's a cultural holiday you are after, then India and to a lesser extent Japan takes some beating. However if push comes to shove because of my love of big game and wild animals Kenya would get my vote.

Maisie

Oscar

Dan & Dylan

Carlea

Ben&Nikki

Rudie and Lottie

Favourite Family Photo

16
AND FINALLY

Just recently I have been hit with a spate of deaths of dear friends. Firstly, Keith who I played squash and racquet ball with every week for 30 years. He lived in Exeter and we would regularly go out together in Torquay after squash, he would then stay over with me. We had a competition we called the Steak Stakes, where the first person to win twenty-one games would have a steak meal bought for him. When four of us went to Spain to play golf on one hole he said, "That's Julian's ball over there, that's Derek's ball there, and that's Barry's ball there, who's is the other ball??" (I think Keith was losing it a bit).

The following year Ray died, he was the fines secretary for Devon Dumpling Golf Society and was really good at it. One day when playing with him we got to the eighteenth and his putting throughout had been dreadful, so I said, "I've just noticed you've got some shite on the end of your putter." He looked under the putter and I said, "No, the other end." He chased me all the way back to the clubhouse. He lived with me for a few weeks when he left his wife.

John S who used to come away with us on golfing trips died very suddenly. His wife asked if the six of us who he used to go away with would be the pallbearers. I was away at the time which on reflection was a good thing because the other five pallbearers were all around six feet tall.

The one that hit me the hardest was the death of Mike Cox, known affectionally as Coxy, who has been mentioned many times in this book. I shared a room with him in Portugal, went to Zambia with him, but he left me a great legacy. He built the house I live in.

Fortunately, now all my children and their families have moved down to the West Country. Daniel and Claire were already in Exeter, Leanne and Joe moved down from Brighton to Whimple and Ben and Nicky moved from Shoreham by Sea to Pinhoe, Exeter, which is great because I can see so much more of them and their children. I adore all my grandchildren, Maisie, Oscar, Dylan, Carlea, Rudi, and the latest addition Lottie. I only have to see one of them and I have a smile on my face for the rest of the day.

ONE REASON FOR LEANNE AND JOE MOVING TO EXETER WAS for them to buy Little Oldway and Leanne to run it which they have now done. Leanne has brought Little Oldway into the twenty-first century and is doing well.

Ben was being made redundant and I suggested he come to work at Oldway Heights which he has now done, and is a tremendous asset to the company. He is now my operations manager with a view to becoming a director, although I cannot see me ever retiring, with him on board this gives me even more time to enjoy golf and holidays.

As I said I am never happy unless I have got a project on the go. I recently completed a project to renovate a flat in Torquay. I do it in conjunction with a builder/bricklayer who arranges all the work and I finance the project. On selling we split the profit, and because he works to an extremely high standard it turns out to be a quality flat. Another project with the same setup is on the go in Exeter.

The house in Florida was put in my children's name, but because of the travelling distance it was hardly ever used. My children had implied that it would be better to have a larger holiday home nearer so I decided to sell. This was a really difficult decision as I really loved going out there and had made many good friends however, all good things come to an end. The two-bedroom apartment in Spain wasn't big enough and the decision to sell that wasn't so difficult. So they both were sold to buy a bigger house in Spain.

I looked at many towns up the coast but as I like contemporary design, I could not find anything suitable. The only ones I found were built around golf courses which were miles out of town. I then looked on Rightmove and saw a house in Los Alcazares, although not contemporary I really liked it so I arranged a viewing and flew out. The house was perfect but right next to it was a huge unfinished building which looked like a six-storey car park so that was no good. Whilst driving with the estate agent I saw a poster and a sign advertising these beautiful contemporary houses, so I said to him, "That's what I want." He took me to see them, but they were two or three miles out of town.

My remit to the agent was a contemporary house within walking distance of shops, restaurants and pubs, and preferably near a beach. As I really liked the town of Los Alcazares and a friend of mine, Rob and his wife Kay from Torquay had recently moved there, I felt that was where I wanted my holiday home. However, there was no house in town which I liked so the only alternative was to build my own. Next objective was to find some land, there were a few plots available but the one I liked was a corner plot of a good size. It ticked all the boxes and was only a two-minute walk from the beach, the downside was it had no views whatsoever and not the best of outlooks, but nevertheless I bought it. I found a brilliant architect who set about designing. I now have a beautiful five-bedroom house with my own swimming pool.

For some time, I was getting out of breath just doing simple tasks like putting the dustbins out, so I went to the heart specialist who arranged a stress test. As a result of the test I was told I would need three stents but because one of my arteries was twisted, he could not put one of the stents in and I would have to go to Plymouth for a heart bypass. Not being happy about this I found out about a stent specialist who worked at London Bridge Hospital and arranged an appointment. I went to see him the following Monday and he told me he could do all three stents. I went back on Thursday, had the three stents put in and back home Saturday. I must admit this is one of the perks of having private health insurance.

Friends are an important factor in my life and I would like to thank the following:-

Pete Baines, Ray Baldwin, Jim & Val Banks, Jayne & John Bastafield, Chris & Ros Bater, Dave & Ann Berridge, Cherry Bradbury, Richard & Sue Brinsley, Tony & Sue Brinsley, Phil & Di Bristow, Pete Buxtorf, Jeff & Barbara Chandler, Larry Collings, Annie Cox, James Cross, John & Carol Dart, Mike & Sue Davey, Chris & Bev Davis, Lionel Digby, Mike & Gill Douglas, Jeff & Joan Easterbrook, Roy Fewster, Sarah Ford, Paul & Gill Green, Jack & Irene Grievson, Tony & Ger Gerney, Doug & Pat Harris, Maggie Harris, Andy Hayes, Rob & Kay Harvey, Jeff Hewett, Paul Howard, Karen Howard, Chris Hucker, Davy & Di Jones, Dave & Heather Klinkenberg, Leanne & Joe Knowles, Kieth & Sarah Mason, Norman & Lyn Lindon, Richard & Bev Madge, John & Sally McKillop, Dawn & Arthur Milford, Bev Nicholas & Karen, James Nicholas & Catherine, Lucy Nicholas & Tom, Chris & Sarah Pallister, Phil & Libby Porter, Ben & Nikki Privett, Dan Privett, Claire Privett, Jackie Privett, Roger & Ross Privett, Lennie & Shellie Pym, Simon & Nikki Rice, Sheila Rice, Pauline Roach, Mike &

Julie Shord, Barry & Mary Smart, Wayne & Joe Stamenkovic, Alan & Gina Tucker, Pete & Judy Vincent, Chris & Mary Walker, Jan White, Andrew Wilshire, John & Rose Woollacott and of course not forgetting my nieces and nephew, Tamasyn, Jodie, Lisa, Nicky, Tracey, Allana and Curtis.

So here I am in the twilight of my life. What is still on my bucket list? Firstly to see my children all reach their goals in life, stay healthy and to see all my grandchildren grow into adults everyone is proud of.

Regarding travelling I still would like to go to South America, Galapagos Islands, Sri Lanka and New Zealand, also a trip on a steamboat up the Mississippi from New Orleans to Memphis would be nice. Other than that, I hope to spend more time in my new house in Spain, especially during the winter months. Clearly none of this can be done until COVID-19 is taken care of but at the time of writing this there is a light at the end of the tunnel. I did know one person who at the very start of the pandemic succumbed to it, but everyone else including the residents of Oldway Heights have stayed clear.

I am pleased with what I have achieved in life so far, mainly three great children and six beautiful grandchildren with financial achievements coming a distant second. After reading this book I hope the expression "It's alright for you" is no longer in your vocabulary, and I look forward to writing a follow-up book in twenty years time.

CPSIA information can be obtained
at www.ICGtesting.com
Printed in the USA
LVHW070338101121
702934LV00001B/4

9781912680481